# Choosing Daughters

D0675436

Rodrigo

# Choosing Daughters

*Family Change in Rural China*

**Lihong Shi**

Stanford University Press

Stanford, California

Stanford University Press
Stanford, California

Printed in the United States of America on acid-free, archival-quality paper

Library of Congress Cataloging-in-Publication Data

Names: Shi, Lihong, 1976– author.
Title: Choosing daughters : family change in rural China / Lihong Shi.
Description: Stanford, California : Stanford University Press, 2017. | Includes
    bibliographical references and index.
Identifiers: LCCN 2016051133 | ISBN 9781503600898 (cloth : alk. paper) |
    ISBN 9781503602939 (pbk : alk. paper) | ISBN 9781503603004 (ebook)
Subjects: LCSH: Rural families—China. | Sex of children, Parental preferences
    for—China. | Daughters—China—Social conditions. | Family size—
    China. | Social change—China. | China—Rural conditions.
Classification: LCC HQ684 .S553 2017 | DDC 306.85/20951—dc23
LC record available at https://lccn.loc.gov/2016051133

Typeset by Motto Publishing Services in 11/13.5 Adobe Garamond Pro

# Contents

# Illustrations

# Acknowledgments

THROUGHOUT THE PROCESS of conducting research and writing this book, I have accumulated many intellectual and personal debts. First of all, I am deeply grateful to Lijia villagers who have to remain anonymous. They welcomed me into their homes, shared with me their stories, and taught me about village life with generosity, kindness, and laughter. I especially want to thank my two host families who provided me with a home during my multiple field trips. A few officials kindly allowed me access to the birth-planning documents of the township and introduced me to the women's leaders in the township.

My deepest gratitude goes to Shanshan Du. Shanshan has been the strongest supporter for this research project and has generously offered her valuable insights and critiques throughout the entire process of this project. With her integrity, compassion, kindness, and love, she has been an inspiring mentor for my intellectual growth and a genuine friend during times of personal crisis. This book would not be possible without her wholehearted support, constant encouragement, and practical advice. I am also indebted to Judith Maxwell and Allison Truitt at Tulane University, who read an earlier version of this book and offered me valuable suggestions.

I have benefited from many productive discussions with colleagues and friends. In particular, I want to thank the following colleagues who read various versions of parts of the manuscript and offered their insights: Geoff Childs, Vanessa Fong, Wade Glenn, Stevan Harrell, Bill Jankowiak, Gonçalo Santos, Priscilla Song, Michael Szoni, Rubie Watson, and Robert Weller. Portions of the book were presented at Brown University, Case Western Reserve University, Columbia University, Goethe University, Frankfurt am Main, Harvard University, Max Planck Institute for Social Anthropology, Shenyang Normal University, Tulane University, Washington University in St. Louis, and at the annual meetings of the American Anthropological Association, the American Association of Chinese Studies, Association for Asian Studies, the Population Association of America, and the Society for Medical Anthropology. I thank the audience for their comments and questions that helped me clarify and sharpen my arguments. I especially want to thank Iwo Amelung, Stevan Harrell, Marida Hollos, Nicole Newendorp, Gonsalo Santos, and Wu Shixu for inviting me to present my research. At Stanford University Press, Jenny Gavacs was very supportive, encouraging, and helpful. I am also grateful to James Holt, Kate Wahl, Olivia Bartz at the press for their assistance. I thank Carolyn Brown and Gretchen Otto for their skillful editorial assistance. Special thanks go to an anonymous reviewer and Bill Jankowiak who offered me insightful comments and valuable suggestions.

My colleagues in the Department of Anthropology at Case Western Reserve University have offered me generous support to guide me through my journey as a new faculty member while I was completing this manuscript. In particular, I thank Melvyn Goldstein and Larry Greksa for their valuable advice and generous support. At Washington University in St. Louis where I was a postdoctoral fellow, I thank Geoff Childs, T. R. Kidder, and Carolyn Sargent for their mentorship, encouragement, and support. Special thanks go to Bob Canfield, a mentor and role model in many ways. Bob offered me tremendous support with genuine care, candid advice, and weekly prayer meetings. I am grateful to Huma Ahmed-Ghosh, a mentor during the early years of my graduate studies, for her long-term support for my interest in studying gender relations in China. Last, my grandfather, who introduced me to Lijia Village, has always been a strong supporter for my intellectual pursuit. My mother stayed with me briefly during my first three field trips. I thank my family for their understanding, patience, support, and love.

The research for this project was supported by summer research grants from the department of anthropology at Tulane University, a research grant from the Newcomb College Center for Research on Women at Tulane University, a research grant from the department of women's studies at San Diego State University, and a research grant from the Wenner-Gren Foundation for Anthropological Research. Writing and revising of this book was supported by three fellowships from the Andrew Mellon/American Council of Learned Societies and an An Wang Postdoctoral Fellowship from the Fairbank Center for Chinese Studies at Harvard University. I thank the above institutions for their financial support that made the research and the completion of the book possible.

Portions of chapter 4 and chapter 5 have been previously published as "'Little Quilted Vests to Warm Parents' Hearts': Redefining Gendered Performance of Filial Piety in Rural Northeastern China," *The China Quarterly*, 198 (2009): 348–363, © SOAS, University of London, published by Cambridge University Press, reproduced with permission; "'The Wife is the Boss': Sex-Ratio Imbalance and Young Women's Empowerment in Marriage in Rural Northeast China," in *Women and Gender in Contemporary Chinese Societies: Beyond Han Patriarchy*, edited by Shanshan Du and Ya-Chen Chen, 89–108, New York: Lexington Books, 2011, reproduced with permission; "From Care Provider to Financial Burden: The Changing Role of Sons and Reproductive Choice in Rural Northeast China," in *Transforming Patriarchy: Chinese Families in the Twenty-First Century*, edited by Gonçalo Santos and Stevan Harrell, Seattle: University of Washington Press, 2017, reproduced with permission. All photographs were taken by the author.

# Choosing Daughters

# Introduction

IN 1983, WANG JING, a woman who was from Lijia Village and who married into a neighboring village, was targeted by local birth-planning officials for sterilization surgery because she already had two daughters.[1] Her family lived next to the village government building, and she could hear it very clearly when the village head announced her name through the loudspeakers for education meetings, organized for women who were required to have sterilization surgery. Because her husband was the only son of his family, whenever they heard the announcement, her widowed mother-in-law would cry that the Lu family (her husband's family) would be finished without a grandson. To fulfill her mother-in-law's desire for a grandson and their own desire for a son, Wang Jing and her husband decided to defy the government mandate and have a third child. They had to run away from their village and move multiple times to avoid a confrontation with birth-planning officials, who were determined to prevent them from having an unauthorized birth. In 1985, after hiding in a town outside their province for a few months, they finally gave birth to a third child, a son. They sent a letter to her mother-in-law, with a photo of their son, to share the good news. But her mother-in-law did not believe them and insisted that they had lied to her to please her. Wang Jing and her husband returned home when their son was nine months old. The moment when they arrived home, her mother-in-law took their son, put him on bed, and opened layers of blankets and clothes. When she finally saw with her own eyes that the baby was indeed a boy, she was so happy that she burst into tears.

Around the same time, a very different story was taking place in Lijia Village. In 1980, when the one-child policy was initiated in the village, a couple named Li Liang and Zhao Yan gave birth to their first child, a daughter. Encouraged by the local government with incentives of an extra piece of land and a small amount of monthly monetary reward, they applied the following year for a one-child certificate (*dusheng zinu guangrong zheng*), a pledge with the government not to have a second child. In 1986, the one-child limit was relaxed to allow rural couples whose first child was a girl to have a second child. Li Liang and Zhao Yan were among the first group of Lijia couples who were granted a second-birth permit. Over the next few years, they seriously debated whether they should have another child. Eventually, to the surprise of other villagers, they decided not to take advantage of the modified policy and gave up their second-child permit. Li Liang and Zhao Yan were the first couple in Lijia Village who voluntarily chose to have a singleton daughter (only one child, a daughter) rather than take advantage of the policy. Following their example, an increasing number of young Lijia couples made the same decision to forgo the new policy and limit themselves to a singleton daughter. In 2006, twenty years after the implementation of the policy that allowed rural couples whose first child was a girl to have a second child, choosing to have a singleton daughter had become widely accepted in Lijia Village and the township area.

Wang Jing's story reveals China's long-standing tradition of preferring sons and the strong resistance of rural couples to the implementation of China's massive and pervasive birth-planning policy (*jihua shengyu zhengce*), designed to limit family growth and consequently the opportunity to have a son. The stories of couples like Li Liang and Zhao Yan, by contrast, suggest significant shifts in reproductive preferences and the increasing appreciation of girls. This book offers a detailed ethnographic account of this emerging reproductive pattern in rural China, where a noticeable proportion of young couples have willingly accepted a singleton daughter rather than take advantage of the relaxed birth-planning policy to have a second child. The book focuses on the complex decision making of these couples in regard to their life goals and childrearing aspirations, changing family dynamics and gender relations, and parent-daughter ties, which have engendered the transformation of reproductive preferences.

## The Birth-Planning Campaign and China's "Missing Girls"

Control over population and reproductive activities has been a crucial component of state governance among modern nation states (Browner and Sargent 2011; Ginsburg and Rapp 1991; Greenhalgh 1994; Kligman 1998). But no population policy matches China's birth-planning campaign in both the scope and intensity of policy enforcement. This unprecedented birth-planning campaign was strengthened in the 1970s, when the Chinese leadership was eager, after ending decades of political turmoil and international isolation, to develop the national economy and considered population growth an immense barrier to modernization. The profound threat of a large population size to economic growth legitimized the implementation of the most massive and stringent population policy in modern human history. Thus, in 1979 a nationwide one-child mandate was implemented in China (Greenhalgh 2008; Greenhalgh and Winckler 2005; Scharping 2003; White 2006), with exceptions applied to couples under certain circumstances (Shi 2017).

To enforce its ambitious and often unpopular policy throughout the country, the Chinese state introduced a set of enforcement measures, including building a multilevel birth-planning bureaucracy to enforce the birth limit, education campaigns targeting a deeply rooted childbearing preference for a large family with at least one son, provision of contraceptive services and mandatory contraception, close surveillance of couples who had not yet achieved their reproductive goals, monetary incentives and punishment that closely linked reproductive choice to an individual's socioeconomic well-being and career advancement—and, when all these measures fail, the extreme measure of forced sterilization and abortion (Banister 1987; Greenhalgh 1994; Greenhalgh and Winckler 2005; Huang and Yang 2004; Potter and Potter 1990; Scharping 2003; Shi 2014; White 2006).

The pervasive and intrusive policy aimed at limiting family growth is, however, in direct conflict with the long-standing tradition of a preference for multiple children and for at least one son among Chinese families. In China's patrilineal kinship system and the Confucian belief and practice of filial piety, a son is expected to offer his parents financial support and nursing care in their old age (Baker 1979; Freedman 1970; Hsu 1948). In addition, a son is essential to passing on the patrilineal family line and practicing ancestor worship. A daughter, however, joins her husband's patrilineage upon marriage. Her filial obligation is thus transferred to her parents-in-law, and she is of no value to the continuity of the patrilineage of her natal family (Du 2011; Knapp 2005; Tan 2004; R. S. Watson 2004; Wolf 1972). Because a son is economically responsible for offering old-age support and culturally significant for continuing the patrilineage, producing at least one male heir has been one of the most significant life goals among Chinese families (Hsu 1948; Wolf and Huang 1980).

Consequently, when the strong desire for a son clashed with the pervasive state campaign to limit family growth, couples who had not yet achieved their reproductive goals persistently resisted policy enforcement. The strategies for resistance varied under different circumstances. The most defiant form was open confrontation with birth-planning officials, such as destroying crops on their family land and damaging their houses to retaliate and even engaging in physical violence (Greenhalgh 1994; Wasserstrom 1984; White 2003, 193–99). More evasive forms of resistance included fleeing and hiding during unauthorized pregnancies to avoid detection by birth-planning officials (Anagnost 1995; Croll 2000, 82–82; Potter and Potter 1990, 241–42; Shi 2014; White 2006, 173–77) and illicit removal of intrauterine devices (IUDs) (Greenhalgh 1994; Wasserstrom 1984; White 2003, 180). Some couples circumvented the policy by devising plans to have one more child, for instance, by bribing medical personnel to issue a false certificate of a child's congenital defects so that they would be allowed to have another child and engineering a false divorce so that an unauthorized pregnancy would be allowed (Greenhalgh 1994; Shi 2017; White 2006, 179–81).[2]

Perhaps the most controversial form of resistance was the gendered practice of infant abandonment and sex-selective abortion. Hoping for a son, some couples adopted out an unwanted daughter and some even abandoned a female infant, so that they would be allowed to have another child (Johnson 1996, 2016; Johnson, Huang, and Wang 1998; Weiguo Zhang 2006). Since ultrasound technology became widely available as a way to determine a fetus's sex and abortion became easily accessible in the 1980s in China, the hunger for a son under strict state reproductive control led to the most violent form of resistance—the abortion of female fetuses (Chu 2001; Murphy 2003; Zeng et al. 1993). This "unnatural selection" (Hvistendahl 2011) has caused a male-biased sex ratio at birth in China (Chu 2001; Murphy 2003; Zeng et al. 1993). According to the official statistics in China, in 2015 China's sex ratio at birth was 113.5:100 (NBSPRC 2016). Although this ratio is much decreased from previous years, it is still beyond the normal range.

The long-term female deficit has led to growing concerns with China's "missing girls" (or "missing women)," a term coined by economist and Nobel laureate Amartya Sen (1990) to refer to a male-biased sex ratio in the developing world, notably India and China (Anderson and Ray 2010). Despite that the Chinese government has designed and implemented a series of measures to prevent sex-selective abortion and has even criminalized health practitioners who collaborate with couples in such practices, the long-term consequence of a male-biased sex ratio has created a marriage squeeze, resulting in millions of men who face the prospect of not being able to marry during their lifetime. The Chinese government has estimated that by 2020 the number of men between the ages of twenty and forty-five will be thirty million more than the number of women in the same age group in China (Jiang 2007). International observers are alert to the potential problems an imbalanced sex ratio can cause. Human rights activists are worried about an increase of trafficking of women and sex slavery, and some alarmists have even warned of the threat of a large number of unattached bachelors to domestic stability and international security (Hudson and den Boer 2005; Hvistendahl 2011).[3]

The increasing concerns with China's "missing" and abandoned girls and the potential consequences of a female deficit have turned media attention and academic studies to searching for the roots of the problem. Inside China, continuing discrimination against girls in some regions has been closely associated with a lasting backward and rural preference for sons, whereas the international community has blamed the draconian state control over population for the suffering of Chinese girls (Loh and Remick 2015). While discrimination against girls, manifested by the practice of female infanticide in the past, had become a marker of a backward Chinese culture in the nineteenth century (King 2014), economic development, technological advances, and state governance in modern times have not improved the lives of Chinese girls; on the contrary, they have exacerbated the plight of these girls.

## An Emerging Reproductive Pattern of Choosing a Singleton Daughter

This book focuses on an emerging pattern of rural couples' choosing voluntarily to have a singleton daughter. This choice is particularly surprising because the birth-planning policy, since the mid-1980s, allowed these couples to have a second child and thus a chance to have a son. More strikingly, these couples have shown great appreciation of and affection toward their singleton daughter and have supported that daughter in an unprecedented manner. This book does not attempt to deny the gender-biased reproductive practice that still persists in some regions in China. Instead, it tries to bring to light a critical yet largely overlooked reproductive pattern emerging in China's demographic landscape. While discussing the diversity of reproductive behaviors in China, Judith Banister (1987) has stated: "A common problem in the study of huge countries like China is the tendency to deal only in the aggregate, ignoring the variety and complexity of subnational experience. Yet, better understanding of the regional and even the national picture can be derived from a look below the surface" (251). This book is thus an attempt to look "below the surface" of the diverse and complex reproductive choices in China to reveal the new pattern and transformations within rural Chinese families that have engendered the new reproductive pattern.

Rural families who have voluntarily chosen to have a singleton daughter are officially recognized as *dunuhu* (household with a singleton daughter), a phrase introduced by the state birth-planning bureaucracy. These families have decided to forgo the opportunity to have a second child that the policy provided for rural couples whose first child was a girl. This reproductive choice has been documented in Shandong Province (Liu and Ding 1993), Zhejiang Province (Xinmei Huang 1994; Rong Zheng 2004), and Jiangsu Province (Li 2009) in East China, Hubei Province in Central China (Ci and Tian 2004; Hong Zhang 2007; Zhou and Zhou 2001), and Liaoning Province (Mu et al. 2009) and Heilongjiang Province in Northeast China (Yan 2003). Along with this reproductive pattern, a low fertility rate and a relatively balanced sex ratio at birth have also been reported (Xinmei Huang 1994; Mu et al. 2009; Hong Zhang 2007; Zhou and Zhou 2001). Ethnographic studies on changing childbearing practices in rural China have mentioned the choice to have a singleton daughter. In Heilongjiang Province, a "new fertility culture" had emerged by the late 1990s, in which a large number of villagers willingly accepted only one child, and some couples were even content with a singleton daughter (Yan 2003, 200–203). Similarly, in Hubei Province in Central China in the early 2000s, as a feature of new fertility trends, some families had voluntarily chosen to have only one daughter (Hong Zhang 2007).

Recognizing and responding to this new reproductive pattern, the Chinese government in several provinces has recently begun to provide financial aid to elderly couples who have a singleton daughter. For example, in 2008, the government of Jilin Province in Northeast China initiated a pilot program to provide rural couples who had a singleton daughter with an old-age security fund (Jilin Provincial Government 2008). Several other regions—for instance, Hubei and Guizhou Provinces and the Chongqing metropolitan area (Huang and Zhang 2015; Tai and Li 2015; Zhao 2014)—have implemented a preferential policy in college admission for singleton daughters as rewards and incentives for rural families with a singleton daughter. In Hubei Province the policy was first enforced in 2009; in 2014, 15,862 singleton daughters from rural families had benefited from the policy (Huang and Zhang 2015).

The emerging reproductive pattern among rural Chinese couples who choose to have a singleton daughter reveals two distinct transformations of reproductive preference among rural Chinese families. First, instead of adhering to the large family ideal, these couples have chosen to have only one child. Second, and more strikingly, by voluntarily forgoing the opportunity to have a second child, a chance for a son, these couples have diverged from the long-standing belief that holds sons indispensable. The pattern of choosing a singleton daughter has emerged under massive and stringent state control over population growth. This choice thus coincides with rather than contradicts state-mandated fertility norms. Although state promotion of a small family ideal and the value of girls has played a significant role in the decision-making of young Chinese couples, acceptance of a singleton daughter is a grassroots choice, the result of their pursuit of a modern family, a successful child, and an intimate parent-child bond rather than a passive response to the draconian state reproductive governance.

The reproductive choice to have a singleton daughter involves a decision-making process. When young people reach the important life stage of married life, they learn to be wife and husband, daughter-in-law and son-in-law, and mother and father as their families grow and as they take on new family responsibilities. Meanwhile, these young people have to constantly adjust their desires and adapt to changes in the communal and societal environment, including rising consumption and changing gender dynamics. Their decision to have a singleton daughter is thus a consequence of continuous responses to their changing family responsibilities and transformed social, economic, and cultural environment—to "the diverse flows of conduct of which fertility is composed" (Carter 1995, 83). This book delves into the various forces behind the complex decision-making process of these couples to reveal a desire for a small family and a divergence from the long-standing tradition of son preference in China.

## The Research Community

The field research for this study was conducted in Lijia Village and the surrounding township area. Lijia Village is a multi-surname village in Liaoning Province in Northeast China (see map). In 2007, Lijia Village had a population of eight hundred in 265 households.[4] Although Northeast China hosts the largest number of Manchu ethnic minorities in China, the majority of residents in Lijia Village and the county area are

Map of Liaoning Province

Han Chinese. According to the village household registration records, among all Lijia residents in 2007, except for five Manchu, six Hui, and fourteen Mongolian, the remaining of residents were Han Chinese. After hundreds of years of ethnic interaction, there were no distinct differences in the beliefs and the lifestyles between the few ethnic minorities and the Han villagers.

Lijia Village is about four kilometers away from the seat of Dacheng County and another ninety kilometers away from Shenyang, the capital of Liaoning Province. The village is one among eighteen administrative villages in Yangshu Township. Because the township government is located adjacent to Lijia Village, villagers are within walking distance of a primary school and the only township middle school as well as the township administrative offices and service centers such as the medical clinic and birth-planning clinic. The village government serves as an intermediary between villagers and the township government. The basic functions are to disseminate government policies and manage village affairs—for example, by allocating land and mediating disputes among villagers. The village government is mainly composed of the Communist Party secretary and the village head, the two highest positions in the village. In addition, the leader of the Women's Federation (women's leader, *funu zhuren*) is responsible for the implementation of the birth-planning policy and other issues related to women. Another important position is an accountant who is in charge of financial affairs of the village government.

Lijia Village is bordered by a highway that connects the village to the county seat and neighboring villages and townships. Public transportation and local taxis are available from early morning until early evening. It takes about ten minutes by bus to travel from Lijia Village to the county seat. Long-distance buses to Shenyang and neighboring counties run on a daily basis along the highway. In addition, a large number of villagers have purchased motorcycles or electric bicycles to travel to the county seat, their work place, and their relatives' homes in other villages. The close proximity to the county seat and the accessibility of transportation have offered great convenience for Lijia residents to take employment outside the village, visit relatives, and shop in the county seat.

The village witnessed migration to Northeast China during late imperial times, Japanese occupation and the civil war in the first half of the twentieth century, the radical political movements during the socialist period, and the subsequent economic reforms. During the middle of the seventeenth century, the county area was designated by the Qing court as a local administrative office, which served as a transit center and a post house. The area was later populated by migrants from the other side of the Great Wall, who settled in the region and made a living by farming. Following the Japanese invasion in Northeast China in 1931 and the establishment of the puppet state Manchukuo, the county area was under the governance of the Japanese. In 1945, immediately after the Japanese surrender, civil war broke out in the county area. Between 1945 and 1948, the county changed hands several times between the Communists and the Nationalists before the Communists took over the county in 1948.

The earliest settlers in the village were the Li family, who were Han soldiers stationed in the region by the Qing court. In the mid-nineteenth century, the Wang family, a couple with six sons and two daughters, migrated from Shandong Province in search of better opportunities for survival, and settled in Lijia Village. At the beginning of the twenty-first century, the Wang family and the Li family were the two largest agnatic groups in Lijia Village. By 2007, there were fifty-nine male members of the Wang agnatic group and thirty-seven male members of the Li agnatic group, all of whom were descendants of the early settlers of the two families.

Like many other rural communities in China, elderly Lijia residents had experienced the nationwide movement of agricultural collectivization that started in the early 1950s.[5] During the collective period, Lijia Village was organized into a brigade and was under the administration of a commune. The brigade was further divided into four production teams, and villagers collectively worked on land allocated to their production teams. In 1983, under the decollectivization of agriculture enforced throughout rural China, collective farming was replaced by a household responsibility system, under which Lijia villagers were allocated land and had the freedom to make decisions on farming practices and on taking nonagricultural employment.[6] In the early 2000s, the Chinese state abolished several agricultural taxes to relieve peasants from state-imposed financial burdens.

The major agricultural activity in Lijia Village in 2007 was maize cultivation. Because the township government was located adjacent to Lijia Village, it occupied a large amount of arable land from Lijia villagers. Lijia Village, together with a few neighboring villages, had the least amount of per capita arable land in the township. In 2007, the average amount of land per capita in Lijia Village was 3.7 *mu*, or 0.61 acre, about half the amount in some other villages in the township. The mechanization of agriculture has significantly reduced the demand for farm labor. In addition, during farm seasons, villagers have the option of hiring their fellow villagers to help work on the land. The mechanization of agriculture and the availability of hired labor allow villagers the time to engage in other economic activities.

To supplement their income from farming, some families have engaged in side-line production (for instance, raising cattle and chickens and growing vegetables for sale) and small-scale businesses, such as running a convenience store and selling prepared food to villagers and students in the nearby schools. The burgeoning market economy has also created employment opportunities right outside the village and in the county area. In the early 1980s, a brick kiln was built outside the village, providing jobs for a large number of Lijia residents. In addition, a few factories were also close to the village, including a crushed stone factory and a soy sauce and vinegar factory. In recent years, an economic development zone has been established in the county area, specializing in ceramic tile production. Many Lijia residents work in the factories in the development zone for nine to ten months a year.[7] In addition to these employment opportunities, some Lijia residents work at construction sites, restaurants, and garment factories in the county seat. Some villagers have migrated to the city of Shenyang and other urban areas to work in factories and restaurants. The income from nonagricultural employment and other economic activities has become a significant and indispensable portion of family income.

Lijia villagers practice patrilocal postmarital residence, in which women typically move to their husband's village upon marriage. A few years after marriage, a young couple usually separates from the husband's parents and establishes its own household. Because of the practice of village endogamy, some women are married to a Lijia resident and remain in Lijia Village. In addition, because of the close proximity of Lijia Village to employment opportunities outside the village and in the county area, some married Lijia daughters moved back to the village with their husbands and children a few years after marriage. Like other rural communities in which village endogamy was practiced and affinal ties were strong (Yan 1996), many Lijia villagers form close ties with their affinal relatives.

Unlike in rural Southeast China, where lineage culture has been revived starting in the 1980s when the Chinese government relaxed its control over lineage organizations and religious practices (Chan, Madsen, and Unger 2009; Oxfeld 2010; Yuen, Law, and Ho 2004), Lijia Village has never had a strong lineage culture. Although displaying ancestral scrolls was widely practiced in the past, after the vehement state bans during the Cultural Revolution were relaxed, only a small number of villagers resumed displaying a scroll. While the practice of grave visits has been revived, villagers now visit their ancestors' graves within a nuclear family or an extended family rather than among agnatic group members.

## Project Development and Research Methodology

The research for this book originated from my interest in the education of girls in rural China. Like many Chinese students who grew up in urban areas in the 1980s, I was frequently reminded by mass media and school education that the vast majority of China's rural population was "backward," "ignorant," and "feudal-minded." This "backward" mentality was best exemplified by the perceived universal preference for sons and discrimination against daughters. Rural families without a son were reported to try all means to violate birth regulations to have a son and to reserve limited family resources for sons and deprive their daughters of education opportunities. Media reports on the plight of rural girls can be characterized by a widely circulated poster for China's Hope Project (*xiwang gongcheng*), a governmental charity program initiated in the late 1980s by the China Youth Development Foundation to raise funds to help school dropouts to return to school and improve school facilities in poverty-stricken areas in rural China. The Hope Project's poster—a portrait of a girl with a pencil in her hand and large and innocent eyes full of yearning for knowledge—has moved many Chinese, including me, to donate money to the charity to help support students like the little girl.

When I began a master's program in women's studies, my budding feminist consciousness led me to explore the reality and roots of gender inequality in education in rural China. In the winter of 2002, I conducted short-term field research in Dacheng County and in Lijia Village on girls' education. My preliminary research plan included interviewing government officials, school principals, teachers, and parents. I chose Dacheng as my field site mainly because my grandfather was originally from the county seat and still had connections with a few people in the area. Through his introduction, I had the opportunity to interview an official from the education bureau in the county and two school principals. My grandfather also provided a connection to a Lijia Village family that introduced me to several families who had a daughter. While interviewing the parents, I was surprised to discover that several of the families had chosen to have only a daughter, and the parents expressed their high expectations for their daughter's educational achievement. Their decision to have a singleton daughter even though the revised birth-planning policy allowed them to have a second child, along with their strong support for that daughter, challenged my previous assumption of a universal preference for sons in rural China. Therefore, when I started my doctoral study in anthropology, I decided to return to Lijia Village to further explore the choice to have a singleton daughter and the socioeconomic underpinnings of this emerging reproductive pattern.

I made multiple field trips to Lijia Village and the surrounding county area from 2002 to 2012, including two weeks in the winter of 2002, two months in the summer of 2004, another two months in the summer of 2005, twelve months from August 2006 to July 2007, one week in 2010, and one week in 2012. During my seventeen months of research in Lijia Village, I lived with two host families: one couple in their late seventies (in 2007) and one couple in their mid-thirties (in 2007) who had a singleton daughter. My first host family was from one of the two largest agnatic groups in the village, the Wang family. Because I am remotely related to them through my grandfather, the villagers considered me a relative of this family. My second host family belonged to the other largest agnatic group, the Li family. Both host families were also closely related to some other families through affinal ties. Through the kinship ties and social networks of my host families, I established rapport with a large number of Lijia families. During my early field trips, I worked with a research assistant, a woman in her early thirties, who was a relative of one of my host families and who grew up in Lijia Village. She had only moved out for a short period upon marriage and moved back with her husband to the village later. She was thus well acquainted with most Lijia residents, young villagers in particular. Through her initial introduction, I got to know a large number of young villagers. Because Lijia villagers referred to each other by kinship terms, they addressed me as "older sister," "aunt," or "Xiao Hong" (Little Hong), which is a way to address a junior person in the village.

During my fieldwork, I was invited to many family dinners, a wedding, an engagement reception, and birthday dinners; participated in holiday celebrations and shopping trips; and observed match-making meetings, grave visits, hospital visits, and school visits. I made multiple trips to the city of Shenyang to visit a few Lijia residents who worked in a factory and a restaurant there. I also accompanied my host families to Shenyang, to give the grandson of one host family a tour of a university that he hoped to attend and to take the wife of the other host family to the factory where her husband was working. During my multiple field trips, I tutored several Lijia students and became good friends with their families.

In addition to participant observation, I conducted semi-structured interviews with villagers. In particular, I conducted in-depth interviews with more than forty couples who had a singleton daughter to gather information on their choice and their views and practices concerning childrearing, consumption activities, old-age support, marital relations, and ancestor worship and family continuity. I also interviewed many elderly and middle-aged parents about their views on filial piety and old-age support, childrearing practices, wedding financing, ancestor worship, and the enforcement of the birth-planning policy. Because some topics could be sensitive, I tried to conduct individual interviews. For example, when I interviewed elderly villagers on their views on filial piety, I only interviewed them when their children were not present. I also interviewed some men and women separately on topics related to marital relations.

I administered a household survey with 248 couples of reproductive age (women under the age of fifty) in Lijia Village and a neighboring village, focusing on family size and composition, their decision on whether to have a second child, residence patterns, their views on old-age support, and their expectations for their children's education. In addition to interviews and surveys, I also conducted research at the township archive to collect fertility records in the township and local birth-planning policies.

To understand the reproductive pattern in a broader context, I interviewed the women's leaders from fourteen villages in the township in addition to the women's leader in Lijia Village. I collected birth information for residents in these villages by going through the village household registration records with these women's leaders. I also collected birth information in three other villages in the township from the birth-planning records collected by the township birth-planning office.

In addition, I made multiple trips to four villages neighboring Lijia Village in the township, where I interviewed some residents about their reproductive choice. Throughout my fieldwork, I was able to receive assistance from a few birth-planning officials in the village and the township, possibly because of my ties to my host families, who were relatives of some of these officials, and also because my research focused on couples who had chosen not only to comply with the birth limit but also to accept a singleton daughter, which the officials would regard as the "bright" side of the birth-planning campaign. I was able to conduct multiple interviews with the women's leader and former women's leader in Lijia Village, as well as two officials from the township birth-planning office. The director of the birth-planning office in particular kindly offered me critical assistance, including granting me access to the township archive twice and introducing me to the women's leaders in other villages in the township.

I was not, however, received positively by the village head and the Communist Party secretary in Lijia Village. They were unwilling to talk with me in detail about village affairs. I only talked a few times, briefly, with the village head, who did kindly allow me access to the village household registration records. Although unwilling to have in-depth interviews with me, they were not hostile to my presence in the village, and I enjoyed the freedom to conduct my research without the interference of the officials throughout my fieldwork.

### Overview of the Book

Chapter 1 discusses the formulation and implementation of and reactions to the birth-planning policy in Lijia Village to present a local account of the practice and the experience of China's population control campaign. The chapter first explores the evolution of the birth-planning policy, various measures of the implementation of the policy, and the diverse responses to policy enforcement among rural couples. As an increasing number of rural couples accepted the policy, starting in the 1990s, a new reproductive pattern emerged in which couples willingly embraced a singleton daughter despite the implementation of a relaxed policy that allowed them to have a second child.

The following chapters delve into the social, economic, and cultural forces underpinning the emerging reproductive pattern. Each chapter focuses on a critical factor to unravel the complex decision-making process of couples considering whether to have a second child. Chapters 2 and 3 focus on factors contributing to a preference for a small family, in this case, only one child, among young Lijia couples. Chapter 2 examines how the burgeoning market economy and the retreat of the state in governing the social life of villagers have facilitated the formation of a new ideal of happiness, defined by material consumption and the enjoyment of leisure. As a result, young villagers have come to believe that child-rearing jeopardizes the pursuit of their new life ideal and thus are likely to decide not to have a second child. The chapter concludes with a consideration of the burden of childrearing on young women and of their reproductive agency in choosing to have only one child.

Chapter 3 explores the changing childrearing strategy among young couples and its impact on reproductive decisions. Corresponding to their belief that raising one successful child is more rewarding than raising multiple unsuccessful children, many young couples have chosen to concentrate limited family resources on only one child to secure the best possible upbringing. The chapter examines parental support for a child's daily consumption and education, with a particular focus on daughters to demonstrate that the childrearing beliefs and practices are no longer gender specific. This gender-neutral parental support has contributed to the acceptance of singleton daughters.

Chapters 4, 5, and 6 focus on factors contributing to a decline in the preference for sons and their impact on the decision to accept a singleton daughter. Chapter 4 examines the gendered transformation of filial piety and its impact on reproductive choice, first exploring the arrangements of elder care and the radical transformations of the gendered practice of filial piety, in which support provided by sons and daughters-in-law has declined while married daughters have proven to be more filial. The chapter then turns to the socioeconomic underpinnings of this transformation: the reinterpreted logic of intergenerational relations, the emerging filial practice of married daughters, and the shift of post-marital residence and women's socially constructed role as being more considerate than men. The decline of filial support from sons has weakened young parents' desire for a son; in addition, young couples have started advance planning for their old age, including cultivating a close bond with a daughter.

Chapter 5 delves into the burden of financing a son's wedding and its impact on the decision to embrace a singleton daughter. The chapter first examines the significance of marriage to men and the increasing financial burden on the groom's family of financing a wedding, which has trapped many rural families in severe debt. Further, a male-biased sex ratio in the marriage market has given young women the upper hand in negotiating marriage proposals and has further increased the cost of wedding financing. The chapter also explores the long-term planning and preparation for wedding finance and the continuing support for a son after his marriage. The chapter closes with a discussion of the impact of the burden of financing a son's wedding on reproductive choice. The dramatic shift of the role of sons from providing security in old age to becoming a financial burden has further encouraged couples to willingly accept a singleton daughter.

Chapter 6 turns to the eroding effect of the belief that family continuity depends on having a son. Because of its lack of a lineage culture, Lijia Village has no institutional support for the belief and practice of having a son to pass on the family line. Further, skepticism regarding the belief in an afterlife and a reciprocal relationship between the ancestors and the living descendants has shaken the religious and cultural significance of having a son to perform ancestral rituals. Finally, financial ability has replaced family continuity as the most significant marker for social status, thus removing the stigma attached to families without a son. In the process of emerging from the "ancestors' shadow," young couples are more willing to embrace a singleton daughter.

The book concludes with a discussion of the implications of this emerging reproductive pattern on the understanding of family transformations in rural China in general and son preference in particular, as well as the ways in which this new pattern sheds light on studies of state-society relations in reproductive choice and control in China.

# 1

## The Birth-Planning Campaign
*Local Experience of Population Control*

CONTROL OVER POPULATION SIZE has been central to China's population politics since the founding the People's Republic of China in 1949. The massive birth-planning policy to limit family size was strengthened in the 1970s when the Chinese state designed strict measures to enforce the birth limit. Since its implementation, the policy has drawn considerable academic attention as well as heated political controversy in the international community. Although many Western observers have severely criticized the draconian policy for state intrusion into private personal affairs and the coercive measures of policy enforcement, the Chinese government has claimed the policy's success as measured by a declining birth rate. How then has such a pervasive and invasive social engineering project been carried out among the Chinese populace? How has the policy been received by the Chinese populace?

This chapter focuses on the birth-planning campaign in Lijia Village from the 1970s to 2010, offering a local account of the practice and the experience of China's population control campaign. While unfolding the ways in which the pervasive policy was implemented and received on the local level for more than three decades, this chapter reveals that as the policy was adjusted and relaxed and implementation measures modified, the reactions of the villagers toward the policy were transformed. More strikingly, with an increasing number of peasant couples accepting the policy starting in the 1990s, a new reproductive pattern emerged, in which couples willingly embraced a singleton daughter rather than take advantage of the relaxed policy that allowed them to have a second child.

## Policy Formulation and Revisions

During the early years of the People's Republic of China, the Chinese leadership considered a large population to be a valuable labor force for socialist economic development and nation-building and continued its earlier pronatalist policy in the 1930s and 1940s to encourage childbearing (Tang 2005, 53–54; White 2006, 20). Like the Soviet policy that honored women who gave birth to a large number of children with the title "Mother Heroine" and monetary rewards (Mitsuyoshi 2012), the Chinese government encouraged women to aspire to this motherhood ideal. Women who produced a large number of children were praised and rewarded. In Lijia Village, several elderly villagers recalled that at a township meeting, government officials gave high praise to a Lijia woman for having nine children and even rewarded her with some cloth to make clothes for her large family.

The pronatalist population policy was short lived, however. In the mid-1950s, with rapid population growth, tight food supplies, and an ambitious economic development plan, the government formally took a step to promote birth control to slow down population growth (White 2006, 26–32). Since then, the Chinese leadership has enforced an antinatalist birth policy in varying degrees of intensity, with short periods of interruption during two radical political movements in the 1950s and 1960s, i.e., the Great Leap Forward and the Cultural Revolution (Greenhalgh and Winckler 2005; Scharping 2003).

In the countryside, birth-planning work began in the mid-1960s and was intensified in the 1970s (Greenhalgh and Winckler 2005; White 2006). In the early 1970s, a nationwide "later, longer, fewer" (*wan, xi, shao*) campaign was launched, in which couples were urged to marry late (twenty-three years of age for females and twenty-five for males in rural areas) to delay childbearing, wait longer between births, and have fewer children (Tang 2005, 111–25; White 2006, 59). The 1970s witnessed the strengthening of the birth-planning campaign as the birth quota was further restricted. The tightened policy allowed each couple to have only two children, spaced several years apart. Lijia villagers who had experienced the birth-planning campaign during that time could still recall the well-known slogan on the birth limit: "two children per couple, four or five years apart" (*yidui fufu yiduihai, lianghai xiangge siwunian*). Meanwhile, policy enforcement was intensified. Couples who had two or more children were required to undergo sterilization surgery.

Toward the end of the 1970s, a national one-child policy was taking shape, and in 1979–80 the one-child limit became official state policy (Greenhalgh 2008), enforced on the majority of Chinese families, with exceptions applied to families under certain circumstances (Shi 2017).[1] Since its initiation, the one-child policy has been modified and relaxed a few times. In 1984, in response to strong peasant resistance, the central government adjusted the birth limit in rural areas by opening a "small hole" (*kai xiaokou*) to allow couples under certain conditions to have a second child (Greenhalgh and Winckler 2005, 113–16; Scharping 2003, 58–63). In Lijia Village, two couples were granted a second-child permit under this policy adjustment. In one case, the wife's widowed mother had four daughters and no sons. The relaxed policy allowed the couple to have a second child because the couple was committed to support the elderly mother. The husband in this type of arrangement was officially referred to as *yanglao nuxu*, meaning a son-in-law providing old-age support for his parents-in-law. In the other case, in which a couple was allowed to have a second child, the husband's only brother was a childless bachelor in his forties.

In 1986, the birth limit was further relaxed in some provinces, including Liaoning Province, to allow rural couples whose first child was a girl to have a second child (Zeng 1989).[2] A couple needed to meet the requirements for spacing between the two births and a minimum age for the mother. When the policy was first initiated in the township in 1986, a couple was allowed a second child when the first child had reached the age of three and the mother was at least thirty-one years old. In 1986, the minimum age for the mother was modified to twenty-nine. In 2003, the age limit was further relaxed to twenty-six, and the spacing requirement was abolished. A couple was required to apply for a second-birth permit through the women's leader, who delivered the required form to the couple and instructed the couple to submit the form to the county Bureau of Population and Family Planning. When the application was approved, the wife could go to the birth-planning clinic at the county seat to have her IUD removed.

Toward the turn of the century, China's total fertility rate had declined well below the replacement level (roughly 2.1 births per woman). Meanwhile, the demographic consequences of the birth-planning policy were looming large. With a growing aging population that depends on family for support and a skewed sex ratio at birth, further relaxation of the birth limit seemed inevitable. Thus, in 2003, the Chinese government took a further step to allow a couple to have two children if both spouses were singletons themselves. In 2013, the policy was further relaxed to allow couples to have two children if one spouse was a singleton.[3] These policy revisions eventually led to a nationwide two-child policy for all couples, announced in late 2015, thus ending the decades-long one-child birth limit.

## Policy Implementation: From Education to Coercion

To ensure that the strict and often unpopular birth-planning policy is successfully enforced among Chinese families, the Chinese government has designed and implemented a series of measures for policy enforcement, covering various aspects affecting reproductive decision making and behavior, such as promoting the use of contraceptives, providing education aimed at changing childbearing preferences, and exerting control over the economic and social well-being of a family. Correspondingly, the severity of enforcement measures ranges from propaganda to the most violent forms of coercion.

### The Creation of a Birth-Planning Bureaucracy

When the policy was designed, an ad hoc multilevel birth-planning bureaucracy was established for policy enforcement. At the top tier of this state agency, the National Population and Family Planning Commission was assigned major administrative tasks, including formulating population targets, setting policy implementation guidelines, and training birth-planning personnel (Huang and Yang 2004).[4] Below the state level, birth-planning offices were established at each government level—province, city, county, township, and village (or district, street, and residential committee in urban areas)—with each level holding its subordinate offices responsible for meeting the population targets set by their superiors through a set of specific measures.

In Lijia Village, the Communist Party secretary and the village head are in charge of the overall enforcement of the policy. In addition, the women's leader is responsible for enforcing the policy according to the guidelines from the township authority.[5] She is assigned two assistants to help her implement the policy.[6] The major responsibilities of the women's leader includes informing villagers of the birth policy, assisting the township office with contraceptive service delivery, facilitating villagers' applications for a birth permit or a one-child certificate, and monitoring women of reproductive age (15–49) to make sure that they do not have an unauthorized birth. During the early years of the policy enforcement, the township government organized short-term campaigns and recruited local activists to help with birth-planning work, such as searching for couples who had run away to avoid sterilization or abortion. Working at the very bottom level of China's massive hierarchical birth-planning network, these grassroots cadres and activists formed the backbone of the pervasive birth-planning campaign. Because they were often long-time and active members of their village communities, they were well aware of the reproductive preferences, financial conditions, and extended family and social networks of their fellow villagers. Their familiarity with the reproductive preferences and the social and economic well-being of their fellow villagers enabled them to tacitly engage with targeted villagers for policy enforcement.

Beyond the village, there is a family-planning office in the township. Its administrative responsibilities include collecting demographic data from the villages, informing women's leaders of policies and implementation measures, and delivering contraceptive services through a birth-planning clinic located at the township government headquarters. In the county, the Bureau of Population and Family Planning oversees the enforcement of the policy in the county area and offers a wider range of services through its birth-planning clinic.

To hold local birth-planning officials accountable for policy enforcement, the birth-planning bureaucracy established an evaluation system that imposed administrative and financial punishment on officials who failed to meet the birth-planning target and rewarded those who successfully enforced the policy. This evaluation system was later developed into a nationwide "one-vote veto" (*yipiao foujue*) system that included an appraisal of enforcement of the birth-planning policy into the evaluation of the overall job performance of an official, even setting it as the primary criteria (Greenhalgh 2010, 50; Huang and Yang 2004; Shi 2014; Weiguo Zhang 2002, 51). Officials who failed to meet the designated birth-planning targets might severely jeopardize their career, making them ineligible for promotion and bonuses, and might even lead to job loss. For example, according to a township government document issued in 1985, for one unauthorized second birth in a village, the birth-planning personnel would each be fined 150 yuan. They would each be rewarded with fifty yuan, however, if there were no unauthorized births and no coercive abortions in the village. In 1993 the fine was increased to five hundred for two unauthorized births and the village party secretary had to resign for failing to enforce the policy.

### Delivery of Contraceptive Services

Once a birth-planning bureaucracy has been established, one of its major tasks is to deliver contraceptive services. In each township, a birth-planning clinic was set up to offer free contraceptives. Available contraceptive methods for women include IUDs, tubal ligation, oral and injectable contraceptives, Norplant, and spermicide; condoms and vasectomy are available for men. The birth-planning clinic at the county offers services such as abortions for unauthorized pregnancies and free IUD removal for women who have been granted permission to have a second child.

During my fieldwork, married couples of reproductive age who had one child or more were required to use some type of contraceptive method. Among the majority of couples, the wives took responsibility for birth control. Before 1998, when sterilization was required for couples who had given birth to two or more children, in almost all cases the wife had tubal ligation surgery. No vasectomies were performed in Lijia

Village. I heard of only one case from a neighboring village in which the husband had undergone a vasectomy. Women who had only one child were required to have an IUD inserted. Newly married women were not required to use birth control. After a woman gave birth to her first child, however, the women's leader was required to remind the woman to have an IUD inserted three months after a vaginal birth and six months following a cesarean delivery.

### Education, Persuasion, and Inspection

In addition to offering contraceptive services, another major task of the birth-planning bureaucracy is to enforce the birth limit through education on the policy and to maintain surveillance of women of reproductive age. Broadcasting and slogans are used to educate villagers. Many Lijia villagers recall that during campaigns in the 1970s and 1980s, trucks with loudspeakers patrolled the village to propagate the policy and promote enforcement. In addition, birth-planning slogans were painted on the walls of village government buildings and walls around villagers' yards. The slogans closely associated childbearing with the well-being of a family and the development of a nation. One slogan painted on the wall surrounding the township government building in 2001 was still recognizable in 2007: "Have fewer and higher quality births to benefit the country and the people" (*shaosheng yousheng, liguo limin*) (fig. 1). Another slogan painted on the wall around a family's yard in a neighboring village said: "We strongly encourage each couple to have only one child" (*dali tichang yidui fufu zhishengyu yige haizi*) (fig. 2). Similar slogans, such as "For the prosperity of the country and the happiness of the family, please plan your births" (*weile guojia fuqiang, jiating xingfu, qingnin jihua shengyu*), could also be found on the walls along the highway bordering the village (fig. 3).

While information about the policy was publicized in the village through propaganda, education meetings became a more powerful way to deliver the policy to each family. Organizing education meetings was more frequent in the late 1970s and the early 1980s, when birth regulations were intensified. All couples who had expressed a desire for more children and women who were targeted for sterilization surgery were

**Figure 1.** Birth-planning slogan painted on the wall of the township government, 2007. The slogan says, "Having fewer and higher quality births to benefit the country and the people."

**Figure 2.** Birth-planning slogan painted on the wall around a family's yard in a neighboring village, 2004. The slogan says, "We strongly encourage each couple to have only one child."

**Figure 3.** Birth-planning slogan painted on the wall along the highway bordering Lijia Village, 2004. The slogan says, "For the prosperity of the country and the happiness of the family, please plan your births."

required to attend the meetings. When a meeting was scheduled, loud-speakers in the village announced the names of women required to attend the meeting. The women's leader in Lijia Village during the time told me that she and other officials from the village and the township would read government documents to the attendees at the meetings and explain their responsibility to abide by the policy. She would reiterate the significance and the inviolability of the state policy and would try to persuade the women to comply by emphasizing the burden of raising a big family.

Couples who refused to attend the meetings were subject to economic punishment imposed by the village authority. A couple told me that in 1980 they were targeted to abort the wife's pregnancy because they already had one child. The couple was required to attend education meetings during breaks from work in their production team. If they refused to attend the meetings, their work points would be reduced. During the time when living necessities were distributed by production teams based on an individual's work points, they had no choice but to attend the meetings.

Education became such a crucial enforcement measure that other government agencies, including the education bureau, were required to participate to facilitate the campaign. For example, the textbook for a fifth-grade course called *Shehui* (Society), issued by the provincial education bureau, included the birth-planning policy as one of its topics. In the textbook, the threat of overpopulation to national economic development and the burden on families of raising a large number of children were clearly presented as the rationale for enforcing the policy. Education on the policy became so pervasive that a fifth-grade mathematics textbook included a problem using fertility statistics from the birth-planning campaign.

When such educational measures failed, persuasion became the next step. The women's leader frequently visited couples who were determined to violate birth regulations by refusing to have sterilization surgery or end an unauthorized pregnancy. The women's leader would make multiple visits until the targeted couple finally agreed to comply. When faced with strong-willed couples who tried to evade her, she would deliberately visit after midnight—at 3 am, for instance—to look for the couple and show her determination to enforce the policy. If couples still refused to abide by the policy, officials from the township government would visit them. Frequent visits and persuasion were effective in some cases. A few villagers told me that they had agreed to abide by the policy because they did not want to be confronted in such an intrusive and disturbing manner all the time.

In addition to education and persuasion, inspection was another major method for monitoring couples of reproductive age, especially in the 1980s and the 1990s. Menstruation checks and IUD checks were two major ways to monitor women's reproductive activities to prevent unauthorized births. Lijia women of reproductive age were required to report their menstruation cycles every month to the women's leader or her assistants. The women's leader who worked in the village in the 1980s told me that women whom she believed were likely to have an unauthorized birth became her major targets. She and her assistants would visit these women when their new menstrual cycle was due and would return daily if they did not report the start of a cycle. For women whom they considered untrustworthy, they would even go to the outdoor toilet to check for menstruation pads to verify reported menstruation. One township birth-planning official told me that some aggressive women's leaders even asked women to take off their pants to show their menstruation pads to prove that they were not pregnant. In addition to menstruation checks, a regular IUD check was required for women with two children or with one son. The IUD check was performed at the township birth-planning clinic through an ultrasound examination to make sure that the women's IUDs were properly placed.

*Incentives and Punishment*

The implementation of the policy was also accompanied by incentives for couples who complied and deterrents and punishment for couples who violated the policy. According to official documents and my interviews with villagers, incentives included money, land, and work points and rest periods following a sterilization procedure during the collective era; amounts have varied during different periods since the 1970s. When sterilization was encouraged for couples with multiple children in the early 1970s, women who voluntarily had the surgery performed were praised and rewarded. A Lijia woman who was among the first group of women who had the surgery told me that after the surgery the officials pinned a big red flower, a symbol of honor, on the chest of each woman, and offered them a free meal. Another major incentive was money and land for couples who agreed to have only one child and applied for a one-child certificate. In the 1980s, a couple who had applied for a certificate was rewarded with one *mu* (0.16 acre) of land and fifty yuan each year until their singleton child reached age fourteen.[7] In 2006, the reward for couples with a one-child certificate was ten yuan a month but no land was granted. Since 2005, rural parents who have only one child or two daughters have been granted six hundred yuan a year once they have reached the age of sixty as a reward for abiding by the birth limit and as old-age financial assistance.[8]

Those who violated the policy, however, were subject to financial and administrative punishment, including monetary fines, confiscation of land and properties, deduction of work points, refusal of household registration for an unauthorized birth, and removal from government positions. For example, in 1984 a couple would incur a fine of five hundred yuan for an unauthorized birth. If a couple refused to pay the fine, the township and village authorities had the power to confiscate and sell their house and other properties. For a house that could not be sold, the local government was entitled to dismantle the house and allocate the land to other villagers.[9] During my fieldwork, I did not hear any instance of a house's being dismantled. But in several cases a couple could not afford a fine and had to let the authorities take away property, such as furniture, a clock, livestock, and agricultural products. A woman who had an unauthorized second birth in 1981 told me that the officials "refused to allocate my [newborn] son any land and asked us to pay a fine of 1,500 yuan. We did not have the money. They took our wardrobe, a watch, a sewing machine, corn, and sorghum, all of which added up to 1,500 yuan. If we refused, interest would be added. Years later, when I went to the village government building, I saw my wardrobe still inside the building!" Since 2003, monetary fines have become the major form of punishment, and officials are no longer authorized to confiscate family property for policy violations. A couple is subject to financial penalties that range from five to ten times the annual per capita income in rural areas of the county for one unauthorized birth.

### Coercion as the Last Resort

When all other measures fail, coercion is the last resort. According to my interviews with villagers, between the 1970s and the early 1990s, women who refused to have sterilization surgery or an abortion were taken by force to the township birth-planning clinic for the operation. When couples ran away to avoid a procedure, the birth-planning personnel had the responsibility to locate their whereabouts and take them back to have the operation. A Lijia woman who worked as an assistant to the women's leader in the 1990s told me that during her tenure she was asked a few times to join a team that included the women's leader, the village head, and several officials from the township to look for two

Lijia couples who had unauthorized pregnancies. Neither couple had registered their marriage and applied for a birth permit.[10] During the searches, after the team had arrived at the house where a wanted couple was reported to be hiding, each team member was assigned a spot—for instance, outside a window or in the middle of a road—to prevent the couple from running away. The team, however, was not able to find the couples.

In the 1970s, when the township government organized mass sterilization campaigns, work teams were organized to make sure that all women who were required to have sterilization surgery had complied with the regulation. A Lijia man who participated in such a campaign in the mid-1970s told me that he was assigned to work in another village in the township; officials were exchanged between villages to avoid team members' protecting their fellow villagers. The major task of the campaign team was to enforce sterilization surgeries on couples with two or more children. In preparation for handling couples who might refuse to have the surgery, the campaign organizers assigned at least one male member in each team because of men's relative physical strength. The Lijia man had to travel to other villages to look for couples who refused to have the surgery and hid outside the village. When members in the campaign team were searching for fleeing couples in the neighboring area, the women's leader and other officials from the village offered them information on the couple's possible whereabouts. If someone reported the return of a fleeing couple, the team would try to capture them immediately.

Although coercive measures have never been sanctioned in any official document issued by the central government, birth-planning officials have justified extremely violent methods with the rationale that the peasants are too ignorant and backward to be handled in a more humane way. While local cadres were sympathetic with their fellow villagers because the targets of their birth-planning work were often their relatives and friends, some cadres shared a similar view of couples who were determined to have an unauthorized birth and described them as "old-minded" (*naojin jiu*) and "poorly educated" (*wenhua di*).

Coercive measures during policy enforcement were officially forbidden in the 2001 Population and Family Planning Law. A township birth-planning official told me that they had instead resorted to law enforcement during policy implementation. For a couple who had an unauthorized birth and refused to pay the fine, a law enforcement team from the county Bureau of Population and Family Planning would get involved. In these cases, the husband or wife (usually the husband) would be held in detention until the family paid the fine. A women's leader from a different village in the township told me that the law enforcement team often chose to detain the husband during holidays, such as the Lunar New Year, because no family would leave a loved one in detention during holidays and would try all means to collect the money to pay the fine.

## Peasant Reactions: From Resistance to Acceptance

The pervasive enforcement of the birth-planning policy encountered various reactions from the villagers. When the policy was intensified in the 1970s and was further strengthened with the one-child rule in the early 1980s, implementation of the policy was severely contested, especially by couples who had not yet achieved their reproductive goal. Some couples employed various strategies as a way of resistance, while others developed tactics to negotiate and even collaborate with local officials to fulfill their childbearing desires. After the highly contested 1970s and 1980s, reactions to the birth-planning policy in Lijia Village changed into acceptance, even among couples who had not achieved the traditionally desired family composition with at least one son.

### Resistance

When the birth regulations were tightened in the 1970s, policy enforcement met with varying degrees of resistance, ranging from open confrontation with birth-planning personnel to more evasive tactics similar to the "everyday forms of resistance" adopted by peasants in Malaysia (Scott 1985). Corresponding to the measures employed in policy enforcement, the most frequently adopted forms of resistance can be classified into four categories: open confrontation, fleeing and hiding, passive engagement with birth-planning officials, and aborting female fetuses.

Open confrontation in the form of showing antagonism or even violent assaults has been reported in some regions in rural China where villagers turned their frustration and anger toward birth-planning officials (Mueggler 2001, 311–16; White 2006, 193–99). Although Lijia villagers told me about conversations among a few people about retaliation against the women's leader, I did not hear of any actual physical attacks against birth-planning officials in Lijia Village. Open confrontation with the officials in the area was manifested, rather, by hostility toward and severe verbal conflicts with the women's leaders when, during their home visits, they would try to persuade couples to have sterilization surgery or an abortion. Some Lijia villagers would use insulting language toward the women's leader when the conversation became contentious. The women's leader described the antagonism from villagers she encountered. Once she had even cried during an intense conflict. My interviews with the women's leader in a neighboring village revealed similar tensions. In the late 1970s when she tried to enforce sterilization surgeries on women, she felt that she had become a target of condemnation in her village. A few villagers even spit on the ground to show their contempt when she passed by their houses.

Peasants faced with a powerful state determined to enforce the birth limit often offered more evasive resistance. Fleeing and hiding outside the village was one tactic for escaping the watchful eyes of local cadres during unauthorized pregnancies and required sterilization surgeries. This strategy was so widely adopted by rural couples determined to carry through an unauthorized pregnancy (Anagnost 1995; Chen 2011; Croll 2000, 82–83; Shu-min Huang 1998, 182; Potter and Potter 1990, 241–42; White 2006, 173–77) that these couples have been referred to in Chinese popular culture as *chaosheng youjidui* (excess birth guerrillas). The phrase derives from the title of a popular skit performed by two well-known comedians for the annual New Year's Day show aired on China Central Television in 1990. The skit depicted a rural couple on the run with their three daughters, fleeing birth-planning officials in order to have a fourth child. Some Lijia women mentioned the phrase while sharing with me their own experience of fleeing and hiding. To avoid officials who came to persuade them to have an abortion or sterilization, some women hid during the day and returned home only after dark. One Lijia woman told me: "Once when I saw the women's leader enter the gate, I escaped through the window and hid in the cornfields. Another time my neighbor told me that the women's leader was coming. I left the village and stayed in the county seat."

Since 1980, when the birth-planning campaign was tightened, some couples had to leave their village for an extended period and return only after the birth. The story of Wang Jing (told at the beginning of the introduction) demonstrates the tension between birth-planning officials who were pressured to enforce birth regulations and strong-willed couples who were determined to fulfill their reproductive desires. Wang Jing was targeted for sterilization surgery in 1983 because she and her husband already had two daughters. One evening, she was watching a movie with other villagers outside the village government building of Lijia Village when the movie was suddenly disrupted. She soon found that officials from her village had come to take her back for the surgery. Her father negotiated with the officials and promised to bring her back the next day. The next morning, Wang Jing's father drove her in his horse cart past her village government to show the officials that she was back. Instead of returning home, however, they went directly to a neighboring village to stay with their relatives. Knowing that the officials would soon come to look for her, she and her husband started their journey as "excess birth guerrillas" with their second daughter, leaving their first daughter with the wife's parents. They first settled in a village in a neighboring county but soon found that it was not a safe hiding place when a pregnant woman who was also seeking refuge in their neighbor's house was found by the officials from her village. They then fled all the way to Inner Mongolia Province and rented a house. In 1985, Wang Jing gave birth to their third child, a son. Nine months later, when the police were investigating a theft in their neighborhood, they decided to return to their village because they feared the discovery of their unauthorized birth. When they returned home, they were required to pay a large fine for violating the policy. They were only able to register the birth of their son and obtain a share of land after they bribed a township official so that they could pay a reduced fine. In 2006, while reflecting on her experience of fleeing and hiding, Wang Jing told me: "The villagers often joke with my son about our experience. Someone said to him that 'your mother's experience is enough to write a book, a thick one.'"

The strategy of passive engagement with birth-planning personnel involves showing indifference toward the education of policy enforcement. This tactic was often adopted at education meetings in the 1970s and the 1980s. Villagers sometimes did not actively participate in the meetings: some would be babysitting a toddler, some knitting a sweater, and others even taking a nap. When enforcement of the one-child birth limit began in 1980, two pregnant women were required to have an abortion because they already had one child. When they refused, they were asked to attend education meetings. In one case, the husband would stay at the meetings without uttering a word while the officials made an effort to persuade him to take his wife for an abortion. The officials had to let him go when it was time to close the office in the evening. In the other case, the wife would ignore the officials at the meetings and would instead play cards with other women.

The last category of resistance was the abortion of female fetuses. After ultrasound technology become available during pregnancy check-ups in the 1980s, some couples resorted to aborting a female fetus in order to have a chance to produce a son. Although this "accommodative style of resistance" (White 2006, 207) seems to conform to the birth limit, the motivation behind it is to circumvent the policy in order to have a son. Despite the prohibition of disclosure of the sex of a fetus, some couples bribe a doctor or health practitioner to find out. A woman told me that she and her husband secretly gave the doctor two hundred yuan during a pregnancy checkup in the county hospital and the doctor told them that the fetus was a boy. In a private clinic located in the county seat, the advertisement for ultrasound scans was prominently posted outside the clinic. In 2010, an ultrasound test cost sixty yuan at the private clinic. A Lijia woman told me that the doctor was willing to disclose the sex of the fetus if a patient promised to return for future tests and treatments. Following a pregnancy checkup, abortifacients were available upon a patient's request.

Because of the sensitive nature of this topic, I was unable to collect data on the number of sex-selective abortions by Lijia women and thus cannot report on the frequency of this practice. Only one Lijia man told me honestly that his wife aborted a female fetus before giving birth to a son. Some villagers told me that they knew of women who had aborted a female fetus. While systematic data collection on cases of sex-selective abortion is unavailable, data on sex ratio at second birth suggests that the practice might not have been as prevalent as reported in other regions.[11]

In fact, a few Lijia women spoke of their decision not to abort a female fetus. One woman refused, against her husband's will, to abort a female fetus. In another case, after serious debates, a woman decided to give birth to a girl. This woman already had a daughter, and she and her husband had decided to have a second child, hoping for a son. After obtaining a second-birth permit, she became pregnant. Her most recent ultrasound at a private clinic in the county seat confirmed, however, that the eight-month fetus was a girl. When I visited her, she told me that she had purchased an abortifacient from the doctor the day before. She said: "I had even put the abortifacient to my lips last night, but I just couldn't take it." She debated whether she should abort the fetus. She told me: "If I have an abortion and have another pregnancy, it is not guaranteed that the next child will be a son. But if I keep the child and have a third one, we cannot afford the fine [for having a third child]. Even if we could afford the fine, it is still not guaranteed that a third child will be a son." Two months later, she gave birth to her second daughter.

### Negotiation and Collaboration with Officials

In Susan Greenhalgh's study on the implementation of the birth-planning policy in West China in the 1980s, she documented the ways in which local villagers negotiated with grassroots cadres to reshape official policies on late marriage and birth limits (Greenhalgh 1993, 1994). To conceptualize the negotiation process and the outcome, Greenhalgh (1993) argued that the implementation of the policy went through a process of "peasantization." As is described in Greenhalgh's study, local cadres, employed by the state and yet remaining members of their village communities, often mediated between state mandates and peasant childbearing demands. Consequently, they sometimes made concessions to peasant demands by making minor revisions of state policy.

Negotiation with birth-planning officials occurred in Lijia Village when a few couples were required to have sterilization surgery. In 1980, a Lijia woman was pregnant with her third child and was required to have an abortion. The couple claimed that the wife's physical condition could be in danger if she underwent an abortion. They even demanded that the officials sign a guarantee with them that the officials take full responsibility if the abortion caused physical complications. Because none of the officials dared to take on such a tremendous responsibility, they reached an agreement with the couple that the wife could continue with her pregnancy but had to be sterilized right after her delivery. In a 1991 case, a Lijia woman who had given birth to her second child was required to be sterilized. Unwilling to undergo a surgery, she claimed that she needed to cook for her family and that a surgery would thus not be possible. The women's leader made an agreement with her to cook for her family on the condition that she would have the surgery. As a result, the women's leader and her assistant cooked for her family twice a day for an entire month while the woman was recovering from her surgery.

Peasant couples have also negotiated with birth-planning officials for reduced fines after violating the policy. Wang Jing, the woman who ran away from her village to avoid sterilization, told me that when she and her husband returned to their village after giving birth to a third child, they found that not only her land and her husband's land but also their second daughter's land had been confiscated; the government had refused to register her third child for household registration status and had fined them four thousand yuan.[12] Unable to pay such a large penalty, they bribed an official in the township family-planning office (a woman who was related to Wang Jing's father's agnatic group) and their village officials with gifts, such as bottles of liquor, cartons of cigarettes, and fish. Finally, the officials agreed to reduce the fine to 1,900 yuan and dismiss all of the other penalties.[13]

While officials had to bend policies for strong-willed couples who refused to comply, in a few cases they even collaborated with villagers to help them achieve their reproductive goal. Similarly, when abortion was criminalized in Ceausescu's Romania, sympathetic doctors circumvented regulations to legitimate an abortion for women who were burdened with a large family, engaging in the "politics of duplicity" (Kligman 1998). Within China's birth-planning bureaucracy, the politics of duplicity would occur when officials colluded with their relatives and friends or people who bribed them (Greenhalgh and Winckler 2005, 192; Shi 2017; White 2006, 177–83). Between 1980 and 1982, a few Lijia couples (all from the Zhang's agnatic group) were able to have an unauthorized birth. During that time, the village head was a respected member of the Zhang's agnatic group. The women's leader during that time told me that although the village head promised to help her persuade those couples to abide by the birth limit, he did not take any action. In another case in the late 1990s, a Lijia couple planned to have a third child after giving birth to two girls. Because the wife was diagnosed with hepatitis B, she was given permission not to have sterilization surgery. She had to have three abortions because of close surveillance of the women's leader. In 1998, the women's leader was replaced by a woman who was a close relative of the couple. The wife became pregnant again soon, and this time, without interference from the newly appointed women's leader, they successfully ran away and gave birth to their third child.

### Acceptance

Amid the highly contested reproductive politics of strict state control and strong peasant resistance and tactic negotiation, some Lijia couples willingly accepted the policy and some of its implementation measures. These couples had already achieved their desired number and sex composition of children. Like women in rural Shaanxi who had borne a large number of children in the 1950s and 1960s and supported birth-planning work because of the burden of childbearing and childrearing (Hershatter 2011, 207–8), during the 1970s, when sterilization surgery was required for Lijia couples who had two or more children, some women voluntarily chose to undergo the surgery because they did not want to have any more children. A woman who had two sons and two daughters told me that she was one of the first women in the village to volunteer for surgery: "I wanted to finish early, when the weather was cooler in the morning. I was not like some women who were afraid of the surgery. What is the use of having many children? I definitely had enough." Since the late 1990s, when sterilization surgery was no longer mandatory, the majority of women have been willing to use contraception, usually an IUD, without the persuasion of the women's leader. Some women discussed contraceptive options with the women's leader or the staff who worked at the township birth-planning clinic. Since the mid-1980s, the majority of couples who had one son or two children have accepted the birth limit. As I will discuss in more detail in the next section, starting in the 1990s, a significant number of couples have gradually accepted a singleton daughter, even after the policy was relaxed in 1986 to allow them to have a second child.

The near perfect record of birth-planning work in Lijia Village since 1983 also demonstrates peasant acceptance of the policy. In 1998, 1999, and 2012, there was one unauthorized second birth each year, two of which involved couples who were not registered for marriage. In addition, in 1998 and 2004, there was one unauthorized third birth each year. Despite the unauthorized births, the officials considered birth-planning work in the village successful. In fact, the enforcement of the birth-planning policy in the entire township was recognized by the county government as excellent. As a result, the township government was awarded the title "Outstanding Township in Enforcing the Birth-Planning Policy" (*jihua shengyu xianjin xiang*) for several years in the 1990s and early 2000s.

Although the county government acknowledged the local officials' accomplishments, the current and former women's leaders in Lijia Village and a few women's leaders in other villages in the township attributed their success to the changing reproductive preferences among villagers and the resulting acceptance of the policy. The women's leader in Lijia Village (who started the position in the late 1990s after working as an assistant to the women's leader in the 1980s and early 1990s) told me that compared to her early work, her job now was much easier. She even moved out of the village and lived in an apartment that she and her husband had purchased in the county seat briefly before moving back to the village because they were unable to adjust to the urban living environment. "There is no need to keep a close eye on people anymore," she told me. "They won't have another child, even though you pay them to [*geiqian dou bushengle*]." Although she had been a tough enforcer of the birth limit in the past, she had become a strong advocate for a second child for couples who had a singleton daughter. Out of sincere care, she frequently tried to persuade her relatives and friends who had a singleton daughter to take advantage of the relaxed policy.

### Embracing a Singleton Daughter

When the policy that granted couples with a singleton daughter a second-child permit was first implemented in Lijia Village in 1986, all the Lijia couples who were qualified for a second child took advantage of the relaxed policy, except for one couple who decided to stop with a singleton daughter.[14] According to my interviews with the former women's leader and couples who had a second child during that period, the modified policy was so eagerly received in 1986 that a few couples had to compete for a limited number of second-birth permits for that year. One couple told me that because they were close friends with the women's leader, they were among the first group to be granted a second-birth permit.

Since the 1990s, however, an increasing number of couples have decided not to take advantage of the modified policy and have willingly chosen to limit themselves to a singleton daughter. This emerging reproductive choice is demonstrated by a large percentage of couples who had a singleton daughter and obtained a one-child certificate. According to my interviews with Lijia parents, the monthly monetary reward (10 yuan in 2007) for obtaining the certificate was not a large incentive for their making the decision to have only a singleton daughter. But because the certificate was required to receive the money, once a couple made the decision not to have a second child, they usually applied for a certificate. Therefore, I have used the application for a one-child certificate as an indicator for the choice of a singleton daughter. Although couples with a one-child certificate were allowed to have a second child if they changed their minds, according to my interviews with the village and township birth-planning officials, this practice was very rare. I collected one such case in recent years in which a couple gave birth to a girl in 1999 and applied for a one-child certificate in 2001, only to return their certificate after the wife became pregnant and the couple decided to have the child. The couple later changed their minds, however, aborted the fetus, and reapplied for a one-child certificate in 2008.

In 2010, 165 Lijia couples in which the wife was under fifty had at least one child. Fifty of these couples had a singleton daughter. Thirty-four (68 percent) of them had obtained the certificate. Another couple who had passed the age of forty-nine also had a singleton daughter and had obtained a certificate. My interviews with the thirty-four Lijia couples who had a singleton daughter and had obtained a one-child certificate reveal that only one couple made the choice because of the wife's infertility after giving birth to their first child. A few other couples told me that they decided not to have a second child because the wife was too weak for childbearing, had experienced a difficult pregnancy with their first child, or had miscarried in the past. They also, however, indicated that if they really wanted to have a second child, they would bear with the risk and try to have one. The women's leader also confirmed that the wife's physical condition was not the most significant factor contributing to their decision to limit their family to a singleton daughter. Among these cases, a woman told me about her attempts to have a second child and her eventual decision to stop with a singleton daughter. After two miscarriages, she had had difficulty getting pregnant again. The doctor from a clinic in the county seat suggested treatments with traditional Chinese medicine. Already debating whether she should have another child while her daughter, in primary school, was showing great potential for college and would require financial support for her education, she eventually decided not to have another child.

Table 1 shows the number of Lijia couples who had a singleton daughter and had obtained a one-child certificate between 1981 and 2010. The table shows that in the 1980s only one Lijia couple made the decision not to have a second child. The number of couples who had a singleton daughter and had obtained a one-child certificate did not increase un-

**Table 1** Number of couples who had a singleton daughter and who obtained a one-child certificate in Lijia Village, 1981–2010

| Year | Number of Couples | Year | Number of Couples |
|------|-------------------|------|-------------------|
| 1981 | 1 | 2003 | 7 |
| 1990 | 1 | 2005 | 8 |
| 1991 | 1 | 2006 | 2 |
| 1993 | 2 | 2007 | 1 |
| 1996 | 3 | 2008 | 3 |
| 1998 | 2 | 2009 | 1 |
| 1999 | 1 | 2010 | 0 |
| 2002 | 1 | | |

til the 1990s. During the 1990s, ten couples applied for a certificate. The number increased to twenty-three between 2002 and 2010.[15]

The decision to have a singleton daughter has been accepted and supported in Lijia Village, particularly among young couples. Villagers told me that couples who chose to have a singleton daughter were open minded (*xiangkai le* or *sixiang datong le*). The majority of couples with a singleton son supported the choice. According to my survey with sixty-one Lijia couples of reproductive age who had a singleton son, forty-three (70.5 percent) couples said that they would not have a second child even if the policy allowed them to. Thirty-nine (63.9 percent) of the surveyed couples also said that they would have chosen to have a singleton daughter if their child had been a girl. The same survey in a neighboring village reveals that among forty-one couples with a singleton son, thirty-four (82.9 percent) told me that they would not have a second child even if they were allowed to. Twenty-five (61 percent) couples also said that they would not have had a second child if their child had been a singleton daughter.

This emerging reproductive pattern is not an exception in a broader context. In Yangshu Township, there are eighteen villages, including Lijia Village. I collected data on the number of couples who had a singleton daughter and had applied for a one-child certificate in the other seventeen villages through interviews with the women's leaders in fourteen villages and research on the birth-planning statistics in the remaining three villages. Of the 951 couples who had a singleton daughter in the township by 2009, 541 (56.9 percent) had obtained a one-child certificate. Table 2 shows the reproductive choice of couples whose first child was a girl in the township between 1987 and 2008. The majority of the first cohort of couples took advantage of the modified policy and had a second child in 1987, a year after the second-child policy was implemented. Since the early 2000s, the number of couples who had a second child has decreased. Meanwhile, the number of couples who had a singleton daughter and had obtained a one-child certificate has increased. This stark contrast reveals a trend of peasant couples embracing a singleton daughter in the township area.

The emerging reproductive pattern in which peasant couples have embraced a singleton daughter suggests that sons are no longer indispensable for couples in Lijia Village and Yangshu township. An exam-

**Table 2** Reproductive choice of couples whose first child was a girl in Yangshu Township, 1987–2008

| Year | A | B | Year | A | B |
|------|-----|-----|------|-----|-----|
| 1987 | 82 | 4 | 1998 | 59 | 11 |
| 1988 | 58 | 5 | 1999 | 38 | 13 |
| 1989 | 47 | 4 | 2000 | 41 | 30 |
| 1990 | 45 | 9 | 2001 | 41 | 11 |
| 1991 | 32 | 14 | 2002 | 42 | 29 |
| 1992 | 46 | 9 | 2003 | 22 | 26 |
| 1993 | 56 | 21 | 2004 | 41 | 54 |
| 1994 | 71 | 9 | 2005 | 39 | 98 |
| 1995 | 60 | 9 | 2006 | 30 | 41 |
| 1996 | 44 | 14 | 2007 | 42 | 28 |
| 1997 | 61 | 15 | 2008 | 23 | 25 |

A. Number of couples who had a second child
B. Number of couples who obtained a one-child certificate

**Table 3** Numbers of second births in Yangshu Township, 1987–2008

| Year | Male | Female | Total | Year | Male | Female | Total |
|------|------|--------|-------|------|------|--------|-------|
| 1987 | 37 | 45 | 82 | 1998 | 36 | 23 | 59 |
| 1988 | 31 | 27 | 58 | 1999 | 14 | 24 | 38 |
| 1989 | 26 | 21 | 47 | 2000 | 30 | 11 | 41 |
| 1990 | 28 | 17 | 45 | 2001 | 20 | 21 | 41 |
| 1991 | 15 | 17 | 32 | 2002 | 22 | 20 | 42 |
| 1992 | 29 | 17 | 46 | 2003 | 9 | 13 | 22 |
| 1993 | 30 | 26 | 56 | 2004 | 23 | 18 | 41 |
| 1994 | 45 | 26 | 71 | 2005 | 23 | 16 | 39 |
| 1995 | 28 | 32 | 60 | 2006 | 15 | 15 | 30 |
| 1996 | 27 | 17 | 44 | 2007 | 16 | 26 | 42 |
| 1997 | 37 | 24 | 61 | 2008 | 11 | 12 | 23 |
| Total | 333 | 269 | | Total | 219 | 199 | |
| Sex ratio: 123.8 : 100 | | | | Sex ratio: 110.1 : 100 | | | |

ination of sex ratio at second birth reveals a similar shift in values. Although a male-biased sex ratio is by no means a recent demographic reality in China, an imbalanced sex ratio at birth was aggravated with the implementation of the birth-planning policy. Scholars have attributed a male-biased sex ratio at birth to underreporting of female births, abortion of female fetuses, and female infant and early childhood mortality (Chu 2001; Croll 1994, 199–202; Murphy 2003; Shi and Kennedy 2016; Zeng et al. 1993), an explanation known as the "hidden girls," "ultrasound," and "infanticide" hypothesis (Cai and Lavely 2007, 110). Population surveys have also revealed that the higher the birth order, the more skewed the ratio becomes. According to the *2005 National 1% Population Survey*, the national sex ratio at second birth was 143.2 : 100 in 2005 (NBSPRC 2007). In Yangshu Township, the sex ratio of second birth between 1987 and 1997 was 123.8 : 100 (333 males and 269 females). The ratio decreased to 110.1 : 100 (219 males and 199 females) between 1998 and 2008 (Table 3). Although still higher than the normal range of the ratio, the ratio is much lower than the national ratio.

The relatively low sex ratio at second birth indicates that sex-selective abortion has not been widely practiced in recent years in Yangshu Township, suggesting that the reasons these couples have chosen to have a second child might not necessarily be to have a son. My interviews with couples who chose to have a second child reveal two major factors contributing to their decision. First, the majority of the couples emphasized that an only child without a sibling might feel lonely (*taigu*) and that two children could therefore keep each other company (*yougeban*) and help each other after their parents passed away. Second, these couples believed that two children could share the responsibility of supporting their parents in old age. Thus, their decision to have a second child derived from the practical considerations of providing company and mutual support between two children and their own preparations for old age.

The decision whether to have a second child is by no means a one-time event. In fact, it is a process of decision making, involving a series of discussions and debates, balancing parental aspirations and the perceived financial, physical, and emotional demands of raising a second child. Some couples made their decision early in their marriage whereas others took longer to reach a decision. In the following chapters, I delve into the complex decision making of young Lijia couples to explore the social, economic, and cultural underpinnings contributing to the reproductive pattern of having a singleton daughter.

# 2

## "Life Is to Enjoy"
### The Pursuit of a New Ideal of Happiness

ON A SUMMER EVENING IN 2006, Li Da, a Lijia man in his late thirties, took his daughter for a ride on his newly purchased secondhand motorcycle. They visited a Lijia couple in their thirties who had a singleton daughter. Li Da parked his motorcycle by the window, entered the room, and talked about his new purchase. He then took out his new mobile phone from his pocket. While showing his phone, he also told everyone that his family just installed cable television. After learning that the couple was waiting to hear whether a ceramic tile factory in the county would offer the husband a job before making the decision to buy a motorcycle, Li Da commented: "You don't buy a motorcycle because you need it for your job. You should buy one no matter what! You can ride your motorcycle to the county seat whenever you want to." He then asked the couple about their plan for a second child, and they told him that they had decided to stop with a singleton daughter. "Then all you have is a daughter," Li Da said. "You have every reason to buy a motorcycle." He jokingly continued: "If you didn't have the abortion [a few years ago], you would have had to save money and probably have only two meals a day instead of three." The husband laughed and agreed: "Sure! We would definitely have had to save money." Li Da then said: "Nowadays society is different. You have to learn to enjoy! Don't look down on me because I am poor. I have everything!"

Li Da's consumption choices are particularly interesting because his family's financial situation was below the village average. He actually borrowed money to buy his secondhand motorcycle. Furthermore, none of his new purchases were necessities. He bought the motorcycle to commute to work, visit friends and relatives, and travel to the county seat for shopping and entertainment, instead of relying on a bicycle or local buses for transportation. The mobile phone was added to a landline at home. The cable television simply made more channels available. The purchases merely made transportation and communication more convenient and entertainment and leisure more accessible. Li Da was not alone in making the choices; he followed the latest consumption trends among a large number of young Lijia villagers. His choices and remarks reveal two significant transformations in family life among young villagers. First, the development of a new ideal of happiness has been fostered, which is characterized by the pursuit of material goods and the enjoyment of leisure. The aspiration for the new life ideal is driven by the latest trends for convenience in daily living, entertainment, and status recognition. Furthermore, achieving the life ideal is closely associated with childbearing decisions. Raising a second child increases the cost of living, thus jeopardizing a couple's pursuit of the new life ideal.

This chapter explores the new ideal of happiness and its impact on childbearing decisions among young Lijia couples, focusing first on the socioeconomic context in which young Lijia couples have come of age and how it has shaped the new ideal. After exploring how the pursuit of this ideal is manifested in daily consumption and leisure activities, the discussion turns to the ways in which childbearing and childrearing conflict with fulfilling the ideal, which influences the decision among young Lijia couples to have only one child. Focusing on reproductive decision making among young Lijia women, the chapter concludes with an inquiry into how the gendered division of labor in childcare has impeded their pursuit of the new ideal and how they have been able to carry out their decision to have only one child when their choice does not coincide with their husbands' wishes.

## Life Is to Enjoy

To understand the new ideal of happiness among young Lijia parents, I first identify their demographic characteristics. This group consists of villagers born between the mid-1960s and mid-1980s. Most of them witnessed and experienced the decollectivization of the rural economy and the subsequent market reforms that started in the early 1980s. They have thus benefited from the economic reforms, with the significant increases in household income and standard of living since then. In addition, with the retreat of the state's governance over village social life following the collective period (Li 2009), this generation of villagers has also enjoyed the freedom to make decisions about their economic activities and leisure time.

During the collective period, Lijia villagers were organized to work in production teams and received income based on work points earned. Productivity was low under collective farming, and villagers had little income left after paying their production teams for grain. Under the collective system, consumer goods such as food and other necessities were either rationed by production teams or purchased with coupons in a local government-run shop and in shops in the county seat. Not only was the villagers' purchasing power limited, the range of products available in the market was limited as well. For example, in the mid-1970s a Lijia man needed to make a few pieces of furniture for his son's upcoming wedding. But the only lumber store in the county had a long waiting list, and it was impossible for him to get lumber in time for the wedding. He had to ask a relative living in the nearby city who had connections through his job to buy him some lumber. He took the bus to the city and, with the help of two nephews, carried the lumber back to the village.

Elderly villagers also remember the hard work and lack of leisure time during the collective period. They were required to work according to production team schedules. To complete their assigned tasks, they sometimes had to start early in the morning and finish late in the evening. Some elderly villagers still recalled the slogan for the work schedule during that period: "Start to work as early as three-thirty in the morning and finish work as late as dark in the evening" (*zaoshang sandianban, wanshang kanbujian*). In addition to work in production teams, during political campaigns villagers were required to attend meetings at which village cadres propagated state policies and mobilized villagers for participation. The work schedule and the demand from the state for political participation left villagers with little time for leisure. Elderly villagers told me that only during the winter, when there was no farm work, did some male villagers play poker for entertainment.

During the collective period, the Chinese state also incorporated women into collective farming. Lijia women left their small children in the care of their mother-in-law or older children while they worked in production teams. Women's farm labor was undervalued, however, and women were awarded fewer work points than men.[1] The gendered division of labor continued at home. After finishing work during the day, women had to perform household chores, such as taking care of small children, preparing meals, doing laundry, and sewing for the family. Like women in rural Shaanxi, who recalled exhaustion from farm work and household chores during the collective period (Hershatter 2011), elderly Lijia women complained about the hardships they endured from state-required labor and household responsibilities for their growing families.

The decollectivization of agriculture and subsequent market reforms in the early 1980s engendered two significant transformations in villagers' economic and social well-being. First, the household responsibility system in farming and opportunities to engage in nonagricultural employment have significantly increased household income. Meanwhile, China's burgeoning market economy has provided a wide variety of consumer goods. In Lijia Village in 2006, in contrast to two stores in the entire township during the collective period, there were five family-run convenience stores in the village, and two stores along the highway, which were easily accessible from the village. A few families bought a freezer and sold ice cream bars in the summer. In addition, the markets and department stores in the county seat displayed all kinds of products, ranging from food and clothes to mobile phones, electronic products, and motorcycles. Much like the expanding consumption and entertainment opportunities in Zouping, a county seat in Shandong Province (Kipnis 2016), a large number of restaurants, karaoke bars, and Internet cafés mushroomed in the Dacheng county seat, providing social space for entertainment and for socializing with friends. House building and renovation became very convenient with a brick kiln outside the village, a crushed stone factory one mile away from the village, and two shops along the highway supplying building materials.

Second, the retreat of the state from the social and political domains of village life allowed villagers to engage in economic and social activities of their choice. No longer under the daily schedule of a production team and the requirement for participation in political campaigns, villagers could choose to spend their free time in leisure activities and socializing with their friends and relatives. Unlike villages in some regions in China, where a large percentage of young residents left their community to work in urban areas (Shao-hua Liu 2011; Santos 2017), the proximity of Lijia Village to employment opportunities in the county area allowed villagers to reside in their village and socialize with other villagers during leisure time.

While describing the consequences of decollectivization in rural Jiangsu Province in East China, Huaiyin Li (2009) argues that decollectivization "not only paved the way for the villagers to change themselves from peasants living on subsistence to managerial farmers, business owners, and factory workers, but also made them increasingly aware of their rights and abilities to reorient and achieve their life goals" (291–292). Young Lijia villagers reoriented their life goals toward consumption of material goods and enjoyment of leisure. During my fieldwork, I often heard young villagers expressing this new ideal as "Life is to enjoy" (huozhe weile xiangshou) as they explained their purchases of new items and their desire for leisure.

This ideal is well expressed by a Lijia man in his early forties who had a singleton daughter. During my visit to his family, he discussed the news about the sudden death of a famous Chinese comedian, Hou Yaowen. He had died of heart attack in 2007 at the age of fifty-nine. A successful comedian who became well known through his performance on television, he was reported to have left behind a large amount of money. The Lijia man commented: "The news said that he had a lot of money. So what? He is dead. The money does not mean anything to him anymore." He continued: "I heard the other day that someone I know died of heart attack. He was even younger than I. You have to enjoy life. You won't take anything with you when you die. If you can afford to live in a big house, why live in a small house?"

## A New Lifestyle of Consumption and Leisure

In their pursuit of the new ideal of happiness, young villagers have transformed the consumption practices and leisure activities of rural life. Unlike their parents' generation, who had kept a frugal lifestyle and been content with much improved living conditions, young Lijia couples desired and pursued a much higher standard of living. Their consumption choices have three distinct motivations: comfort and convenience, status recognition, and entertainment and leisure.

Young couples started to buy consumer goods that were beyond basic daily needs and that provided comfort and convenience in their household chores, transportation, and communication. The purchase of kitchen appliances provides a good illustration. While villagers still relied on a wok for cooking, young villagers started to use newly available appliances, such as pancake makers, electric rice cookers, and electric stovetops for use in the summer to avoid the heat from cooking in a big wok.² In 2012, a refrigerator became one of the most fashionable household items that young couples pursued. It allowed villagers to freeze and refrigerate food all year round. These appliances provided a variety of meal choices and transformed the activities of preparing and cooking food.

Many young villagers also bought a motorcycle or an electric bicycle to replace a bicycle. Although public transportation to the county seat and to neighboring villages was available and convenient, a motorcycle enabled villagers to travel according to their own schedules. In addition to a landline phone at home, in 2007 many young villagers owned a mobile phone. Villagers who worked outside the village were able to use their mobile phones to communicate with their family members whenever they wanted. When she was trying to persuade a neighbor to buy a mobile phone, a Lijia woman said that her husband, who worked in the city, talked to her over the phone every night. He was even able to talk while lying on his bed, without being heard by his roommates.

When these products were first introduced, they were not considered daily necessities and were thus luxuries in the context of rural life. With new trends replacing existing ones, however, the categories of necessities and luxuries had been constantly redefined. In 2007, when a large number of villagers owned a basic mobile phone, a smartphone was more expensive and was considered a luxury. At a wedding that I attended that year, instead of a wedding band, the bride gave the groom a smartphone because it was the latest product that young villagers desired. In 2012, many of them had replaced their basic mobile phones as smartphones became more affordable.

Possessing the latest consumer goods also established the status of young villagers as capable consumers who were well aware of—and had the spending power to keep up with—the trends and modern couples who enjoyed the fruits of an improved standard of living and advances in technology. A large number of young Lijia villagers had worked in urban areas for varying length of time and had thus witnessed the "consumer revolution" in China's urban landscape (Davis 2000). They envied the modern living conditions that urbanites enjoyed. A young Lijia woman who once worked in a restaurant in the city told me: "My boss's daughter played the piano. We can't even imagine having my daughter play the piano." Although the villagers envied the urban living conditions, their dream of an urban lifestyle was often shattered by the reality of the institutionalized divide between rural and urban regions and widening economic stratification. As a result, they made an effort to pursue trends that were achievable. When they returned from a job in the city, villagers often bought a few items that were popular in urban areas, such as kitchen appliances and clothes. Others shopped at the department stores in the county seat to look for products that had become fashionable. To keep up with the latest trends, young villagers often budgeted for new purchases. While showing me the new refrigerator and desktop computer that he and his wife had bought the year before, a thirty-three-year-old Lijia man told me that they had completed their purchases for the previous year but had not made a decision about the next new items on their list. He did tell me that they planned to buy a car in a few years.

The desire for status recognition often results in competitive consumption (Adrian 2006). This is especially evident in rural communities where information on family affairs can become public knowledge. Lijia villagers spread news about a family's new purchases through visits and group chats. Sharing this information and commenting on it was a major component of daily socializing among villagers. One day in 2006, a Lijia man came back from his temporary job in the city carrying a juice maker he had bought at a supermarket in the city. His wife made some fruit juice and asked their daughter to take a few glasses to her cousins who lived in the neighborhood. The daughter came back with two cousins and three aunts who wanted to see the new device. That evening, the juice maker was the focus of the conversations in the neighborhood. Other villagers might look down on families who failed to keep up with the most recent trends. In 2006, a sixty-year-old Lijia man bought an electric bicycle, not a common choice among his peers, who still relied on bicycles and local buses for transportation. His neighbor, a woman in her forties, was not impressed by his purchase and commented: "Why not buy a motorcycle? An electric bicycle seems so unfashionable [tu] these days."

To avoid criticism from other villagers, young couples tried to keep up with the latest trends. This often created peer pressure, best exemplified by house building and renovation. A house is a public display of a family's purchasing power and consumption patterns. Indeed, during my interviews, when villagers made comments on the living conditions of other families, the condition of a house was usually mentioned. The story of a couple's house-building decision in a neighboring village demonstrates such peer pressure. The couple had planned to wait to rebuild their house until their neighbors completed building their house. Seeing that their neighbors' new house was larger than average, they changed their original plan and built a house the following year that was the same size as their neighbors'. While sitting in her large new house during an interview in 2006, the wife explained to me: "We live by the street. If we didn't rebuild our house right away, it would be obvious that our house was too shabby in comparison to our neighbors' new house. We hadn't planned to build such a big house. But our neighbors' house was so big. If ours were smaller, people could easily tell from the street and would look down upon us."

In addition to spending for comfort, convenience, and status recognition, villagers also spent a considerable portion of their income on entertainment and leisure, buying products such as a DVD player to watch movies and listen to music and cable television to increase their choice of channels. In 2007, most young couples bought a DVD player with karaoke functions and occasionally sang songs with family members and friends; only a small number of households, mainly made up of elderly villagers, had not installed cable television. In 2012, desktop computers replaced DVD players among the most pursued consumer goods.

Young Lijia villagers listened to music, played video games, and video chatted with their relatives and friends who lived outside the village. Another leisure activity is playing games, such as mahjong and poker. Although the majority of villagers who play on a daily basis are middle-aged and elderly villagers, some young unemployed women also join in to play mahjong after preparing breakfast and sending a child to school in the morning. Some villagers who work during the day also play mahjong after they return home and finish dinner. In the winter, when there is no farm work and when the brick kiln and the construction sites are closed, playing mahjong and poker becomes the major leisure activity among villagers. During my fieldwork, I learned some villagers' schedules for playing mahjong and poker so that I knew the best time to interview them. The games are consumption activities because they involve gambling and monetary transactions. If players have bad luck, they could lose money equaling a full day's pay from work.

Other leisure activities—for instance, socializing with friends and relatives or watching television—do not require money. Villagers who are not employed would visit other villagers during the day. In the evening, groups of villagers gather in or outside a family's house to chat. Villagers, women in particular, would occasionally visit their families and relatives, perhaps their natal parents or a married daughter, outside the village. Since cable television became available, villagers spend a large amount of their leisure time watching television. They follow TV dramas and often discuss the episodes they have watched the previous day with great enthusiasm.

Among young Lijia villagers, the enjoyment of leisure has expanded outside the village, as the entertainment opportunities in the county seat attract young people in the county area and traveling by motorcycle takes less time than it used to on bicycles or buses. In the summer, young couples frequently visit the county seat in the evening to watch group dancing in the public square and buy snacks from street vendors. Some young Lijia men occasionally have dinner at restaurants and visit karaoke bars with their friends. One Lijia man told me that he secretly kept a portion of his salary from his wife so that he could have dinner at restaurants with his friends without asking her for money because she might disapprove of his restaurant expenses. Before desktop computers became affordable, some young Lijia villagers also visited Internet cafés in the county seat to chat with friends and play video games.

## Balancing Childbearing and the Pursuit of the New Ideal of Happiness

With ever-increasing choices and fast-changing trends, the pursuit of material goods requires strong purchasing power. As a result, young Lijia villagers devote their time to hard work to maximize family income. A local phrase refers to working hard for income as *zhuaqian* (grabbing money). When describing a couple's income-earning ability, villagers often said: "This couple is very capable of grabbing money." The phrase vividly encapsulates the villagers' eagerness to accumulate wealth.

In 2006, almost all married Lijia men under forty had engaged in long-term nonagricultural employment. A large number of Lijia women had taken over the responsibility for farm work when their husbands were unable to take time off from work. In addition, many young women were also engaged in nonagricultural employment to increase family income. Table 4 shows the employment status of married Lijia women under forty in 2006. Among the 112 women, forty-one had taken a nonagricultural job, such as working full-time in the brick kiln, in garment and ceramic tile factories, and in restaurants in the county seat for at least three months in 2006. The women were newlyweds who had not yet had a child, those who could receive help with childcare from their parents-in-law or parents, and those whose children were old enough not to require constant supervision. The availability of daycare centers in the village and the county seat also relieved some women from childcare duties during the day, enabling them to pursue nonagricultural employment. Among these forty-one women, six migrated to a neighboring city with their husbands. Instead of seeking employment outside the village, sixteen women ran a small business such as running a convenience store, selling box lunches and snacks at the nearby middle school, growing vegetables for sale in the market, and raising chickens or cattle. Nine women who were not employed in a nonagricultural job took temporary employment inside Lijia Village whenever they had an opportunity, making crafts at home, for instance, or offering labor during farm-

**Table 4** Married women's employment status in Lijia Village in 2006

| Type of employment | Number | % |
|---|---|---|
| Nonagricultural employment | | |
|     Employed in the county area | 35 | 31.2 |
|     Employed in a city | 6 | 5.4 |
| Ran a small business or family side-line production | 16 | 14.3 |
| Temporary labor | 9 | 8.0 |
| Unemployed | 46 | 41.1 |
| Total | 112 | 100 |

ing seasons.[3] Among the forty-six women who were not employed, some had a small child or a child who went to school. They needed to prepare meals when their husbands returned home from work and when their children returned from school in the afternoon. Others chose not to work outside the home and took on the major responsibility for farm work and household chores.

Young couples who are faced with the decision of whether to have a second child thus have to balance childbearing and their devotion to hard work in their pursuit of the new ideal of happiness. Young couples believe that having a second child would greatly jeopardize their pursuit of consumer goods in two ways. First, as I will discuss in chapter 3, childrearing practices among young couples require considerable financial resources for a child's daily needs and education. Therefore, having a second child would significantly weaken a couple's spending ability. A thirty-year-old man explained his and his wife's choice to stop with a singleton daughter: "We decided not to have a second child because we don't want to lower our living standard after adding the large financial burden of raising another child." Second, young Lijia couples believe that raising a second child also requires a large amount of time, especially during the first few years following the birth of the child. The demand for childcare takes time away from gainful employment, which would limit their earning capacity and purchasing power. Young women explained that if they chose to have a second child, they would have to stay at home for at least a couple of years until they were able to leave the children in the care of their mothers-in-law. As enthusiastic consumers and active participants in the labor force, young women are particularly reluctant to have a second child and miss the opportunity to increase family income.

In his study of economic status and fertility choices among American families since World War II, economist Richard Easterlin (1973) explains how the changing balance between a couple's income earning potential and their desired standard of living influences their fertility choices: "if it is hard to earn enough to support the desired style of life, then the resulting economic stress will lead to deferment of marriage and, for those already married, to the use of contraceptive techniques to avoid childbearing, and perhaps also to the entry of wives into the labor market" (181). Similarly, although the income of young Lijia couples from farming and engaging in nonagricultural employment has significantly increased, driven by rising consumption, they desire a much better standard of living than they currently have. These couples have to balance their income earning potential and lifestyle aspirations in their decision over having a second child. Many were reluctant to compromise their aspirations for the sake of having another child.

Furthermore, young Lijia couples believe that raising only one child affords them the flexibility to work less and gain more leisure time. A middle-aged Lijia woman told me that she and her husband had chosen to limit their family to a singleton daughter. After giving birth to their daughter in 1995, they had planned to have a second child. She herded several cattle and her husband worked in the nearby brick kiln. Her husband, however, was not physically strong enough to take a high-paying but labor-intensive job, and he always felt exhausted after work. One day, while resting on the bed after returning from work, her husband said to her: "Let's apply for a one-child certificate. I am worn out and I really want to quit this job." In 2005, they applied for a one-child certificate.

## Women's Childrearing Burden and Reproductive Agency

The social construction of gender roles in many societies relegates the major parental duty of childcare to women. Burdened by a large number of children, women around the world often complain about the ways in which their childbearing and childrearing responsibilities cause physical fatigue and restrict their mobility and productivity (Browner 1986; Jeffrey, Jeffery, and Lyon 1988; Sargent 2006). Even in pronatalist Chinese society, before modern contraceptive methods became available, Chinese women resented the burden of supporting and caring for a large family (Hershatter 2011), and some even secretly resorted to folk methods of birth control to limit family size (Han 2007). Elderly Lijia women often expressed bitterness about the exhaustion and hardship of bearing and caring for many children and envied the young women nowadays who no longer shared this burden.

Young Lijia women, however, still consider childbearing and childrearing a burden, even with a small family. With their ideal of happiness, these women are eager to engage in employment outside the village to increase their spending power and enjoy leisure time after work. For elderly Lijia women, the desire to limit family size came out of their hope for family survival at a time when they had limited resources for childrearing and when they were subject to the heavy demands of labor at home and in production teams. For young Lijia women, however, the desire for a small family, in this case only one child, derives from their aspirations for family prosperity and enjoyment of leisure at a time when consumption opportunities and leisure activities have become widely available. It is therefore understandable that although young Lijia women are no longer burdened with caring for multiple children, they still consider childrearing inconvenient.

Women who were unable to receive childcare assistance from their mothers-in-law complained about the ways in which their daily childcare responsibilities restricted their opportunities for employment outside the village and their engagement in household chores and farm work.[4] Several Lijia couples had taken a small child with them to the field during farming seasons because they were unable to find a babysitter. Several times they had to look anxiously for a missing child who had walked out of sight in a cornfield while the parents were trying to finish work. A thirty-three-year-old woman who had a singleton daughter spoke of her frustration in trying to finish farm work and household chores while looking after her toddler daughter: "Her father had to work, and I was the only one to take care of her. I could not leave her on the bed for a minute for fear that she would fall. I could not even go to the [outdoor] toilet. I could only prepare meals when she took a nap. But her naps were always very short. Once she fell asleep and I rushed to the kitchen to make pancakes. Fifteen minutes later, she woke up. I tried to hold her with one hand and put corn stalks under the stove with the other hand. But I was not able to. I was so frustrated and angry that I threw the spatula and the pancakes on the floor. When my daughter was older, she always wanted to follow me when I needed to work in the field. She walked too slowly, and I had to wait for her. I was so anxious because I wanted to be able to finish work before dark. It always made me frustrated." She continued: "Whenever I think about all the trouble of taking care of my daughter, I feel that I have had enough."

Women's responsibility for childcare also has limited their opportunities for leisure. A thirty-three-year-old Lijia woman chose to have a second child in 2005 when her first daughter was nine years old. Villagers regarded her as a hard worker who labored alongside her husband at the crushed stone factory outside the village. She was also known as a fan of mahjong and tried to take every opportunity to play, particularly after she came home from work in the evening. After the birth of her second daughter, because her mother-in-law had passed away several years before and her husband worked during the day, she had to look after her newborn daughter all the time. She frequently complained about not being able to play mahjong as much as she wanted because of her childcare duties.

Women who actively participate in the labor force to contribute to the family's income are more likely to limit their fertility because of the conflict between their childrearing responsibilities and their desire to work (Gates 1993; Harrell 1993). The conflict between the tasks of childrearing and working and the enjoyment of leisure have discouraged a large number of young Lijia women from having a second child. Many of these women have received support from their husbands in the decision to limit themselves to a singleton daughter. When they reach a consensus, these couples have usually applied for a one-child certificate within a few years following the birth of their first child. In recent years, a few young Lijia couples had even made the decision before they gave birth to their first child. However, when women's reproductive desire contradicts the childbearing preference of their husbands, they are often able to exercise their reproductive agency to carry out their own decisions.

A plethora of literature has revealed that women are not passive victims of reproductive governance but can be agents in control of their own reproduction (Greenhalgh 1994). Women's agency in controlling their reproduction includes initiating sexual abstinence, negotiating with their husbands to have a sterilization operation, arranging contraception and abortion (Gammeltoft 1999; Kligman 1998; Patel 1999; Sargent 2006), and secretly taking folk medicine for birth control without notifying husbands who want more children (Browner 1986; Han 2007). Since the implementation of the birth-planning policy, Chinese women have to submit their reproductive desires to two competing interests: on the one hand, the Chinese state's claim of control over a woman's reproduction through the massive and intrusive birth-planning campaign; on the other hand, the patrilineal family's desire for a male heir on a woman. Chinese women's agency in defying the powerful state is manifested in their determined resistance to implementation of the policy. In these cases, women have acted "as agents not only for themselves, but also for the patriarchal families to which they belonged" (Greenhalgh 1994, 12). When a woman's desire for only one child coincides with the state's birth limit but is at odds with her husband's wishes, she is able to exercise her reproductive agency through discussion and persuasion.

Some young Lijia women have initiated long-term discussions and debates with their husbands to persuade them to accept a singleton daughter. During their discussions, they would often mention the disadvantages of childrearing, such as the financial and physical burden of raising two children and the unreliability of sons in providing old-age support. After several years of hard work to support a family, the majority of men would agree to the decision, some with great reluctance. When I asked a young Lijia woman about the decision to stop with a singleton daughter, she told me: "We made the decision together. But he had wanted to have a second child. I said to him that it cost too much money to raise two children. We would have to work harder if we had another child. Eventually, he agreed."

When discussion and persuasion fail, some women have defied their husbands' wishes and exercised their reproductive autonomy, as is demonstrated by the story of Xu Hua, who had an abortion against her husband's wishes. Xu Hua and her husband had a daughter in the late 1990s. Her husband always wanted to have a second child, hoping for a son. They shared a yard with her parents-in-laws, and her father-in-law openly expressed his desire to have another grandson in spite of his already having two grandsons from his two older sons. Because Xu Hua's IUD was not properly placed, she became pregnant in 2000. Still in their early years of marriage, Xu Hua and her husband had frequent conflicts. She did not have enough confidence in the marriage and was therefore reluctant to keep the unborn child. In 2006 she confessed: "I debated a lot whether or not I should keep the child. If I had to have a divorce, I could easily remarry with only one daughter. But if I gave birth to a second child and if the child was a boy, nobody would want to marry me [because of the burden of financing a son's wedding; see chapter 5]." She went to the hospital in the county seat alone and had an abortion. When she returned home, her husband and her father-in-law were very frustrated and angry. Xu Hua told me: "It was the October first holiday and we had planned to make dumplings. I was lying in bed to rest. He told me angrily to get up and prepare the dumpling fillings. I knew he was angry because I had aborted the child. I got up and helped to prepare the meal anyway."

Two years later, Xu Hua was pregnant again. Accompanied by a female neighbor, she went to the hospital to have an ultrasound, which showed that she was bearing twins. By this time, her relationship with her husband had been stable and close, and she was not completely opposed to the idea of having two more children. She explained her decision-making process: "I debated a lot after the test, even when I was cooking the next morning. I imagined having three small children lined up on the bed. That was too much [to take care of]. [My husband] didn't mind if we got twins. But I just couldn't accept it." Eventually, she decided to have an abortion. In 2005, her husband finally agreed not to have another child, and she applied for a one-child certificate.

Women's reproductive choices are frequently supported by female friends and relatives who share their preference. Several times, I encountered women discussing their experiences with contraceptive methods and offering other women a pregnancy test. When they went to the birth-planning clinic for an IUD insertion or removal or for a pregnancy checkup, they sometimes went in the company of a female friend or relative instead of with their husband. When Xu Hua was debating whether she should have a second child, a female friend who married into Lijia Village about the same time that Xu Hua had and who lived in the same neighborhood supported her decision to have an abortion and even offered her advice on how to carry out her plan. In an interview in 2007 Xu Hua's friend told me that she "kept telling Xu Hua, why not have an IUD inserted if she did not want another child. She did not have to tell her husband and could just lie to him about it. What does he know? Who do men think they are?"[5]

Unlike women in the past who were only able to exercise their reproductive agency through secret birth control measures (Han 2007), today's Lijia women actively engage in discussions with their husbands on reproductive decisions and openly defy the will of their husbands when they disagree. Women's reproductive agency has been made possible through their emerging empowerment in marriage and in their relations with their parents-in-law. As I will discuss in detail in the following chapters, young women who work have made greater economic contributions to their family's domestic income than in the past. With the sex-ratio imbalanced marriage market, they have also gained the upper hand in forming and ending a marriage. Their empowerment means they no longer need to yield to the authority of their husbands and their parents-in-law and can carry out their own reproductive decisions.

Chinese state's role in women's reproductive agency is more complex. During the implementation of the birth-planning policy, the state imposed the primary responsibility for birth control on women. When the one-child birth limit was enforced, the majority of rural women who had one child were required to use an IUD and those who had two or more children had to have sterilization surgery. Once a couple made the decision to have a second child, usually the wife communicated with the women's leader and prepared the documents required for a second-birth permit. The wife then went to the county birth-planning clinic to have her IUD removed. Women's responsibility for birth control is a double-edged sword: on the one hand, they have to bear the physical discomfort caused by an IUD insertion or sterilization surgery; on the other hand, they are able to take control over their reproductive outcomes. As the story of Xu Hua reveals, when a woman decides not to have a second child, she is able to control her reproduction through birth control or abortion.

## Conclusion

Growing up under China's economic reforms, young Lijia villagers have taken advantage of the consumption opportunities provided by the burgeoning market economy and the freedom to make decisions about their leisure time in their pursuit of a new ideal of happiness. Among many Lijia couples, raising a second child is in direct conflict with the pursuit of the new ideal because childrearing requires financial resources and time away from work and leisure. Many young couples thus have chosen to have only one child so that they can devote their time to hard work to increase their income and to enjoying their leisure time.

Because women still take the major responsibility for childcare, many young women have preferred to have only one child to relieve themselves of the childcare burden so that they can work and enjoy leisure time. While the state birth-planning policy encourages them to pursue this childbearing desire, their empowerment in marriage has enabled them to exercise their reproductive agency and autonomy in their choice to have only one child, even when their husband disagrees. Thus, these young couples, particularly the women, have contributed to China's fertility decline and a new childbearing preference by voluntarily choosing to have only one child.

# 3

## One Tiger Versus Ten Mice
*Raising One Successful Child*

IN THE SUMMER OF 2005, Chen Na, a singleton daughter, was admitted to college, a highly esteemed achievement among Lijia parents and students. Chen Na's parents offered wholehearted support and worked hard to secure adequate income to provide the best possible education for her. Three years earlier, when Chen Na's examination score was below the cutoff for admission to the most competitive and prestigious senior high school in the county, her parents paid an extra tuition fee, referred to as a self-finance fee, to secure her admission.[1] During her senior year in high school, her mother lived with her in a rented room in a house outside her school to take care of her (a practice called *peidu* by Lijia villagers), preparing her meals and washing her clothes, so that Chen Na did not have to live on her own in a school dormitory and could therefore focus on preparing for the college entrance examination.[2] When I talked to Chen Na's mother in 2007 about her move to the school neighborhood, she told me that "it is all worth it. But if we had moved close to the school when my daughter was in her first year in high school, she would have been able to go to a better college."

After Chen Na was born, her parents had debated whether they should have a second child. The financial cost and time required for raising a second child were major factors in their decision-making process. Eventually, when Chen Na became a teenager, they decided not to have a second child. Chen Na's mother explained that the decision allowed the couple to focus their financial resources and attention on their only child, which contributed to her success in securing a college education. If they had a second child, she said, it would be impossible for them to offer the amount of support that Chen Na was able to enjoy. "It is like putting fertilizer on corn plants," she explained. "Suppose you have only one handful of fertilizer. It makes a big difference between putting the fertilizer on three plants and on only one plant."

Chen Na's parents were two among a large number of Lijia parents of their generation who believed in concentrating limited family resources on only one child to secure the best possible upbringing for the child. Their high parental aspirations and strong support for their child's success are similar to the views of Spanish couples in Western Andalusia in the 1980s, who treated their children as "parental projects" and fostered their children's unique abilities to prepare them for success in adulthood (Collier 1997) and of young Palestinian mothers living in Israel whose notion of a proper upbringing required considerable financial and emotional involvement (Kanaaneh 2002). Similar attitudes have been documented among urban Chinese parents who have high expectations for their only child's success and strongly support the child's education (Fong 2004; Kuan 2015; Nie and Wyman 2005) in an effort to cultivate the perfect only child (Milwertz 1997). Not only do young parents in Lijia Village share such attitudes, their childrearing strategies are also closely associated with the decision to have a child. While the pursuit of a new ideal of happiness among these couples has had a significant impact on their decision to have a small family, the new view of childrearing has further encouraged these couples to embrace only one child and, in many cases, a singleton daughter.

This chapter focuses on the new attitudes and practices concerning childrearing and their association with the decision to have only one child. The local notion of success and the belief in the importance of raising at least one successful child, regardless of the child's gender, is examined. The chapter then explores the rising cost of childrearing and the increasing financial investment in a child's daily consumption. The discussion turns to another major source of financial investment in childrearing, a child's education, and examines the local belief in the value of education and the cost of providing it, as well as parental support for a child's educational attainment. Finally, the chapter concludes with a consideration of parental love and support for daughters to reveal the practice of gender-neutral parental support, which further contributes to the embrace of a singleton daughter.

## Defining Success and Childrearing

When describing a successful person, Lijia villagers use the terms *chuxi* (successful) and *younengnai* (capable). They measure a person's success by the socioeconomic status achieved in adulthood. According to Lijia villagers, a successful person enjoys financial affluence and stability, which frees the person from physically demanding and financially unrewarding farm work and enables the person to lead a comfortable and prosperous life. These individuals can achieve such upward mobility either by completing higher education and obtaining a stable job in the city with a retirement pension or by pursuing business ventures. A few Lijia villagers have taken advantage of market reforms and have made sizeable profits running businesses, such as a local brick kiln and a cosmetics store in the county seat. Lijia villagers nevertheless believe that achieving prosperity through business ventures is impossible unless a person is business minded and a risk taker, and/or has close connections with local officials for coveted business opportunities. For the majority of Lijia residents, securing a well-paying, stable job in the city through higher education is a more feasible and reliable option.

According to Lijia villagers, successful people also enjoy higher social status than do peasants, who are often relegated to the lowest rung of the social ladder within China's institutionalized divide between urban and rural regions (Fei-Ling Wang 2005). Villagers of all age groups envy people living in cities with urban household registration status because urban regions are considered more socioeconomically advanced and urban living is associated with a modern lifestyle. Young parents who took temporary employment in the city especially desire living in urban areas. When they are unable to realize this dream, they convey the aspiration to their children.

Lijia villagers believe not only that a successful person enjoys much higher living standards and social status but also that success makes it possible to support parents in old age. With a good income, it is easier to offer elderly parents monetary support. In Lijia Village, several parents with an adult child who was considered successful received continuous financial support and enjoyed much improved living conditions. A few elderly parents were even invited to live with a child's family in the city. The story of a Lijia man's success and his gratitude for his parents' sacrifices was frequently mentioned during my interviews with villagers. All the Lijia residents I interviewed regarded the man as one of the most successful people from the village in recent decades. Back in the 1960s, his parents, who were not able to conceive a child, adopted him. His adoptive parents lived a very frugal life and worked extremely hard to support him through college. Once he became a wealthy businessman, he invited his adoptive parents to live with him and his family in the city. In 2007 the elderly parents returned to Lijia Village for a two-day visit. After seeing that these two former Lijia residents enjoyed their comfortable lives in the city thanks to their son's success and filiality, some villagers expressed to me their admiration for the elderly couple and their belief in the significance of raising at least one successful child.

Young Lijia couples rarely associate the notion of success with gender. Just as parents expect a son to be successful, they have the same expectation for a daughter—an expectation that comes out of parental love. Several parents told me: "A daughter is a child too. Why wouldn't we be happy if our daughter has a better life?" In recent years, a few Lijia daughters have proven to be as successful as their male peers in getting a college and even a graduate education, as well as in securing jobs in the cities. Their educational achievement and career advancement have further encouraged parental support.

Lijia couples also believe that just as a successful son has the financial resources to support parents in old age, a successful daughter will provide as much support as a son does, if not more. My interviews with elderly parents who had both adult sons and daughters revealed that some daughters who had financial security provided even more money to their parents than their male siblings who had limited resources— for instance, paying for a parent's medical bills and offering gift money for a parent's birthday celebration. Several villagers told me the story of a female 1992 Olympic race-walk gold medalist from the county, as an example of the importance of raising one successful child, regardless of the child's gender. According to these villagers, after the success of the Olympian, local government officials visited her parents and awarded them money and a color television set, a luxury for residents in the county during that time, for raising a daughter who brought such great honor to her hometown. A mother, whose singleton daughter knew one of the Olympian's relatives, told me with admiration that she heard that the Olympian bought an apartment in the county seat for her parents. In a separate interview, the father of a singleton daughter told me: "If you have a child like her, it doesn't matter if the child is a son or a daughter."

The hope of raising at least one successful child is vividly expressed in a well-known local saying: "While a tiger can block a road, ten mice are nothing but a meal for cats" (*yizhi laohu nenglanlu, shizhi haozi weimaochi*). According to Lijia parents, it is of no use to raise multiple unsuccessful children who only repeat the fate of being peasants and making a living through harsh farm work and manual labor—a situation equivalent to raising a family of mice whose only value is to feed cats. Raising only one successful child, however, not only secures financial prosperity for the child, but the child is also able to support parents in old age. This practice is equivalent to raising a tiger capable of blocking a road, a symbol for competence and power.[3]

### Childrearing and Consumption

While such parents have high aspirations for their child's success, the cost of raising a successful child, which mainly includes the expense of a child's daily consumption and education, has significantly increased. Because of limited income and supplies during the collective period, Lijia parents were unable to provide a child with abundant material resources. Meanwhile, because the state rationed necessities, all families received the same kind of products. There was little competition among parents to provide the best for their children. Villagers who raised children during that time often said to me: "Every family was the same. We didn't have too much for our children." Since the decollectivization of agriculture and market reforms in the early 1980s, increased income and the availability of a variety of products have transformed the practice of childrearing, particularly parental investment in a child's daily consumption. Consequently, not only has financial support undergone quantitative transformations, with the addition of new categories of products for children, but family expenditure on children has also gone through significant qualitative changes.

The rising cost of a child's daily consumption is first manifested in expenses for food and snacks. In addition to regular meals at home, the majority of Lijia parents pay for school lunches once the child starts preschool, a one-year program before primary school. Around 2000, vendors started to gather outside the township middle school during lunchtime to sell box lunches and snacks to students. The vendors come from surrounding villages, along with a few from Lijia Village. Since box lunches became available, the majority of school children no longer return home to eat, buying their meal from a vendor instead. In 2006, a box lunch cost between one and one and a half yuan.

Although most families can afford the box lunches, parents complain about the increasing cost of snacks, a new category for children's food consumption, which had become an indispensable component of a child's daily diet.[4] Popular snacks include dairy drinks, candies, packaged food, nuts, fruits, ice cream bars, and barbecued food. These snacks can be bought at village stores, the market in the county seat, and street vendors outside the township middle school. During lunchtime and when school is dismissed, street vendors swamp the school entrance and scatter along the street outside with a wide variety of snacks. At home, parents usually give a child pocket money when the child asks for it. Sometimes they ask the child to buy a few items from the village stores and often allow the child to spend the change on snacks. My interviews with young parents revealed that the daily expense for snacks could range from one to five yuan.

Stores owners make an effort to cater to children, purchasing snacks that are popular among children and highly recommended by suppliers, who are well aware of the latest trends. In urban China, television commercials have significantly influenced children's consumption (Chee 2000; Croll 2006a; Yuhua Guo 2000; Naftali 2016, 106), contributing to the "commercialization of childhood" (Davis and Sensenbrenner 2000). Lijia children who watch television commercials are able to follow the same trends as their urban counterparts. While some snacks are beyond the means of the majority of parents, village stores offer smaller or even pirated and cheaper versions. For example, in 2006, a type of dairy drink called Shuangwaiwai, a product from China's largest beverage drink producer, Wahaha, was promoted on television on several channels and soon gained popularity among children who were loyal consumers of dairy drinks. Because a big bottle cost three yuan, which was considered expensive, store owners offered only small one-yuan bottles.

Along with the rising cost of children's consumption for meals and snacks, the cost of children's clothing also has increased. Expenses for childrens's clothing items could range from a few hundred yuan to more than a thousand yuan, depending on the child's age and the parents' spending patterns. In recent years, young parents have been buying brand name clothing for their children. While internationally recognized brand names (Adidas and Nike, for instance) are popular among urban consumers, Lijia parents favor Chinese brands, which have become well known through television commercials and promotions at stores in the county seat. During my visit to a family with a four-year-old singleton daughter, the father showed me a pair of sneakers he and his wife had bought for their daughter a few days before and asked me if I knew of the brand. I told him that I had seen the television commercials. "They cost over a hundred yuan, much more expensive than the shoes sold at the market in the county seat," he told me. "But it is a famous brand and of better quality."

In addition to food and clothing, toys became a new category of children's consumption. A small Lijia child owned at least a few toys, whether dolls, toy guns, toy musical instruments, or a bicycle, which could be bought from street vendors and stores in the village and the county seat. Although small toys were usually cheap and affordable for young parents, large items, such as a bicycle and roller blades, could take a large portion of a family's monthly budget. These toys were unthinkable for young Lijia parents during their own childhood, when toys were usually handmade, simple, and cheap.

Birthday celebrations have become another new category for children's consumption and a trend among young Lijia parents. To celebrate a child's birthday, young parents sometimes take a small child for a photo shoot at a studio in the county seat, a trip that almost all young couples had made at least once. During my visits, parents frequently showed me well-designed photo albums from the child's birthday or hundredth-day celebration. The albums had around ten staged photos in which a child smiled at the camera with toys in his or her hands. In addition to photo shoots, many parents also celebrated a child's birthday with a cake and a special dinner. In 2007, I was invited to a dinner to celebrate a girl's eleventh birthday. A month before, the girl's father had left to work in the city, and he and his wife had promised to buy the girl a cake from a bakery in the county seat for her birthday. The girl's aunt and her two cousins came to visit and gave her a pink sweater as a birthday gift. The girl's mother prepared a meal and invited three more of the girl's cousins to dinner. It was a joyful celebration, and after the dinner the girl expressed her wish for the same celebration the next year.

As young Lijia villagers have been deeply affected by a rise of competitive consumption, they also compete with each other in the childrearing arena. Young parents often boast to other villagers about a new purchase for their children—clothing, for example, or a bicycle. These items make a strong statement about a couple's purchasing power and status as caring and responsible parents, which creates strong peer pressure among parents who feel compelled to follow suit. A mother of a four-year-old singleton daughter told me that she once visited her mother and saw the neighbor's child gliding on a pair of roller blades. After she returned home, she bought her daughter a pair so that next time they visited her mother, her daughter could show off her blades too.

While competitive consumption has significantly increased the cost of childrearing, Lijia children also have developed a strong sense of entitlement, best described by a mother who referred to giving her fourteen-year-old son pocket money as paying him a salary. These children have become full-fledged consumers, well aware of the available products, able to make decisions on purchases, with strategies to achieve their goals. Small children would frequently ask for snacks or clothes, and if their demands were denied, they used crying as a weapon to pressure their parents into buying what they wanted. Parents who lavished affection on their children often gave in to satisfy their children's demands and to avoid becoming the target of ridicule among their peers. A mother of a four-year-old singleton daughter told me that she once took her daughter to the market in the county seat to buy her a dress. When her daughter chose one that was beyond the mother's budget, she suggested a cheaper dress, but the daughter refused to leave and started to cry. Not wanting to give others the impression that she was stingy with her daughter, she ended up buying the dress.

Older children often negotiated with their parents over a purchase. They were aware of their family income, often from conversations between their parents and between their parents and other villagers. A mother of an eleven-year-old girl told me that she once refused to pay for a jacket that her daughter wanted and told her that they did not have the money. Her daughter quickly responded: "My father just brought home money he made in the city. Did you spend it all?" Another mother was speechless when her ten-year-old daughter refuted her claim that she lacked the money to buy her what she wanted. "You played mahjong today [in which gambling was involved]," the daughter said. "Where did you get the money?" When their demands were not granted after their attempts to negotiate, the children would refuse to accept their parents' provisions as a weapon of resistance. An elderly woman told me that her granddaughter felt embarrassed to take homemade food to school for lunch and preferred to buy a box lunch because that was considered trendy among students. One day, the girl refused to eat the steamed buns her grandmother had made and skipped lunch. Since then, her father had to give the girl money for a box lunch.

The availability of a wide variety of products, competitive consumption among parents, and children's demand for consumer goods have significantly increased the expenses for childrearing. According to parents I interviewed, in 2007 the annual expense for a child's daily consumption and other necessities was between 800 and more than 2,200 yuan. This alone could comprised a significant portion of the annual income for a nuclear family with one child (see appendix). The variation in the amount of expenses is first determined by the child's age. Prices for older children's food, clothing, and school supplies are usually higher than they are for younger children's. Parents with teenage children feel increasing financial pressure as their children grow. Another factor contributing to disparities in expenses is the couple's financial status and consumption patterns. While the lowest expenditures could usually be attributed to families with limited financial resources, young parents often strive to reach the highest level of consumption to satisfy their children's demands and demonstrate their status as capable and caring parents.

Some older villagers, however, severely criticized spending so much on one child. They believe that young couples nowadays have much higher incomes than they themselves had in the past, but young couples would still complain about the cost of childrearing because they choose to spend too much on a child. They frequently commented that the expense of raising one child could have covered as many as ten children in the past. An elderly man commented: "Why can't they cut an apple in half to feed two children instead of giving each child an apple? We did it in our days." Young parents would refute such criticism, further claiming that their increased income did not necessarily translate into a stronger ability to raise children, because the cost of childrearing had significantly increased and their children's consumption had become insatiable. While a higher level of income should have enabled a couple to support more children, young couples often make childrearing decisions based on a much higher economic status that they aspire for. Therefore, although these couples acknowledged that their income had increased, they felt, facing the rising cost of childrearing, that their ability to support a large family had diminished.

This reconfiguration of childrearing and the desired family size is prevalent among young Lijia villagers, who often criticize their peers for choosing to have a second child even though they are unable to offer their children a proper upbringing. One day, when I was talking to several Lijia women, a young woman who had a singleton daughter told everyone that she had decided to have a second child. After she left, the other women expressed disapproval: the choice was unwise and irresponsible because, as the result of the woman's relatively extravagant spending, the economic condition of the woman's family was considered below the average in the village. "How is she going to support a second child?" asked one woman. "Begging on the street for food?" In a separate interview, the father of a five-year-old singleton daughter compared his financial support of his singleton daughter with that of some families who had a second child: "We can afford a second child if we really want to have another one. Even the poorest family in the village has a second child. But look at the clothes their children wear and the clothes my daughter and my niece [a singleton daughter of the same age] wear. No child of their age wears better clothes than they do."

### The Cost of Upward Mobility: Parental Support for Education

While the costs of a child's daily consumption are ever increasing, parental support for a child's education and career preparation involves even larger expenses. Lijia parents value education as a way to improve a person's overall well-being. Almost all young villagers attend primary school and middle school, the nine years of compulsory education in China, although some students would stop going to classes in their senior year in middle school when they lost interest in school or when they decided not to continue with a senior high school education. Lijia villages consider people who have a senior high school education and beyond well educated. According to Lijia villagers, well-educated people are polite; they do not get involved in physical and verbal conflicts with others. They are also wise and know the proper way to resolve a family conflict and educate a child. Furthermore, they are intelligent and knowledgeable; they understand the laws and the proper way to protect themselves legally. Finally, well-educated people have social skills that enable them to communicate with others properly.

Lijia villagers often attribute their frustration and failure to a lack of education. A young man who was assigned to operate a measuring machine at his work place told me of his regret for not taking full advantage of the opportunities at school. "My father used to beat me to make me focus on school work. But it didn't work for me. Now I wish I finished at least middle school. At my work place, there is a guy who finished middle school. It is absolutely much easier for him to learn to use the machine." In another interview, a woman with eight years of schooling told me that she was once deceived by a street vendor because she didn't know how to read the scale. She blamed herself for not being well educated.

Some villagers even associate a person's misfortune in life with a lack of education, as is demonstrated by the story of a married Lijia woman from Central China. She met her husband through the introduction of his brother, who once worked in her village. Her story was frequently brought up during my fieldwork, and villagers spoke of their sympathy for her because her husband was considered lazy and abusive. A few years after her marriage, her father sent her a letter, informing her about her mother's critical illness and asking her to return home for a visit. Lacking any formal education, she was illiterate. Unable to read the letter, she asked her husband to read it to her. Fearing that, to escape their marital conflicts, she might decide not to come back once she returned to her village, her husband lied to her about the content of her father's letter, withholding the news about her mother's illness. As a result, she did not return home to see her mother one last time before she died. It was only after she brought the letter to a neighbor that she found out about her husband's deceit. Villagers blamed her misfortune on her lack of education. A Lijia man said to me: "If she had had some education, she would have left her husband. But she can't even read. I bet she doesn't even know how to take the train to go back to her village!"

In addition to valuing education for its significance in improving an individual's overall well-being, Lijia parents regard education as a way to achieve upward social mobility. Deeply rooted in the imperial civil examination system, the cultural model of upward mobility through academic achievement persists in contemporary China (Fong 2004, 101–7; Kipnis 2011). In the past, formal education was a privilege of the elite. The few elderly Lijia villagers who were able to receive primary and middle school education before 1949 were from wealthy landowner families. During the collective period and in the 1980s and 1990s, formal education did become more accessible for peasants. There was little chance, however, for upward mobility through education, mainly because opportunities for college education were highly competitive and parents lacked resources and incentive to support a child's education.

Since the late 1990s, higher education in China has rapidly expanded, and college and graduate education have become more accessible (Bai 2006; Kipnis 2011). Although college expansion has enabled a large number of students to pursue a college education, it has resulted in increasing competition for college graduates in the labor market (Bai 2006). Up until the 1990s, the Chinese state assigned employment positions to college graduates, and every student was almost guaranteed a job upon graduation, whereas the new generation of college graduates has to hone skills, display talent, and compete for employment opportunities in the job market. Students from less prestigious universities and three-year colleges are often considered less qualified, and some are disillusioned by the reality that a college education no longer guarantees promising career prospects. Students who are reluctant to lower their expectations earn a master's degree to gain a competitive edge in the job market. Lijia parents acknowledge that a college education does not necessarily lead to a secure job and realize that their support for a child's education could be a long-term mission. But they believe that without a good education there is no chance at all for their children to improve their prospects. This parallels the belief shared among Spanish parents in the 1980s: "If everyone recognized that schooling did not guarantee a good job, they also recognized that failure to obtain schooling almost certainly guaranteed a bad one" (Collier 1997, 165).

Thus, parental support for a child's education is also based on the pragmatic value of education, which often determines the major that high school seniors choose when they apply to college. Parents and their children often consider such majors as engineering, business, and pharmacy, which they believe will be in high demand in the job market. When students choose to study a science, the student (usually a female student) plans to become a schoolteacher and will often apply to universities that specialize in training school teachers because teaching positions are considered stable and respectable. In fact, I never heard of any Lijia college graduate who majored in the humanities, social sciences, and natural sciences except those oriented toward a teaching career.

Therefore, even though college expansion has been largely funded by increased tuition rates (Bai 2006), which hits rural families the hardest, rural parents are still willing to pay for their children's college education (Kipnis 2011, 35–36; Murphy 2007; Obendiek 2017). High parental support among Lijia parents is revealed in a survey I conducted with 248 couples of reproductive age in Lijia Village and a neighboring village. Not surprisingly, all the couples revealed the high educational standards they hold their children to and expressed their willingness to support their children's education. A number of parents used the expression *zaguo maitie* (to smash a pot to sell the iron) to express their willingness to exhaust family resources to support a child's education. Consequently, an increasing number of Lijia students have had an opportunity to attend college. During the years when I was conducting my fieldwork, at least one Lijia student was admitted to college each year, and a few more students were admitted to the most prestigious senior high school in the county seat (they were all admitted to college later). Additionally, between 2007 and 2012 five Lijia students, after obtaining a bachelor's degree, continued to study for a master's degree; one of them completed his doctoral studies and became the first Lijia resident with a doctoral degree.

Parental support for a child's education starts when a child reaches the age of three and goes to a day care center. The daycare centers in the village and the county seat teach children Chinese reading and writing, mathematics, and even English. The majority of couples send a child to a daycare center so that the child can begin their education. In 2007, seven couples sent their children to the village daycare center, whereas six couples chose one in the county seat. The centers in the county seat cost between 150 and 180 yuan a month in 2007. The cost included tuition, meals, and transportation. Although the center in the village cost only sixty yuan a month, more and more young parents preferred the centers in the county seat because of their well-trained teachers and better facilities. Some parents who sent their children to the village daycare center told me that they planned to send their children to a center in the county seat when their children were older.

Although the cost of tuition for primary school and middle school have been reduced in recent years, parents are required to pay additional fees for textbooks, examination papers, morning classes, and other items. In 2007, the fees added up to around four hundred yuan a year for a primary school student and around six hundred yuan for a middle school student. Parents who expected a child to advance to senior high school usually had to invest more money to help the child compete for the entrance examination. Some parents sent a child to extracurricular classes on weekends and during summer and winter breaks to prepare for courses the following semester. A few parents even spent more than a thousand yuan on an electronic device to help a child learn English. If a child failed the entrance examination for senior high school, the majority of parents would support the child for an additional year as long as the child was willing to try one more time for admission to a senior high school. Parents of middle school dropouts often expressed their disappointment and concern over their children's prospects.

Parents of students in their senior year of high school usually live in a rented room near the school to help the students prepare for college entrance examinations. In 2007, among four Lijia families whose children were in their senior year of high school, three temporarily moved to the school's neighborhood. One of the families had a singleton daughter who had failed the college entrance examination the year before. It was the second year that her parents moved to be nearer to the school. A mother of a singleton daughter who was admitted to college in 2005 told me that during her daughter's senior year, she and her husband spent more than ten thousand yuan on food and rent. In addition, they had to pay almost five thousand yuan for tuition and a one-time nine-thousand-yuan fee for their daughter to be a self-financed student when she started high school.

Once a child advanced to college, parents have to pay a sizable amount for a college education. In 2007, it cost at least fifteen thousand yuan a year for tuition, board, meals, and other necessities. Parents with a child in high school or college were among the hardest-working villagers. To supplement their income from farming, both spouses had to take nonagricultural jobs or run a small business, such as selling snacks to students or growing and selling vegetables in the market in the summer. A mother with a daughter in college told me that her husband's salary as a middle school teacher was barely enough to pay for their daughter's college expenses. She used to stay at home and now had to work in the canteen at her husband's school so that she and her husband would have enough money to support themselves. If a child graduated from college and wanted to go on, parents often supported the child's pursuit of an advanced degree. Several Lijia students tried one more time for admission to graduate school after failing the first time. Their parents supported them for an extra year's preparation for the entrance examination.

While college education is highly desirable to Lijia parents and their children, not all students have the opportunity. Many parents whose children have failed to advance their education or simply lost interest expected the children to attend a professional training school and learn a practical skill—fixing automobiles, for instance, or hairdressing—to improve their chances of securing a job in urban areas or running a small business in the village. These opportunities were viewed as more rewarding monetarily and less physically intensive than farming. During the years when I was conducting fieldwork, a few families paid for a child's training in a professional school after the child expressed interest in learning a practical skill.

### "A Pearl in the Palm": Parental Love and Support for Daughters

Preference for sons and discrimination against daughters in reproductive choice and childrearing were emblematic social practices in the patrilineal and patriarchal tradition in China. When family resources were not sufficient to support a large family, some couples resorted to female infanticide or neglect of girls to ensure that resources went to male heirs, practices that produced higher mortality and lower life expectancy for females than for males (King 2014; Lee and Campbell 1997; Lee and Wang 1999; Mungello 2008). Among wealthy families who had the financial resources to support their children's education, parents had little incentive to pay for a daughter's education because once she married, she was considered a member of her husband's family and her parents did not benefit from their investment in her (Fei 1939; Wolf 1972). One elderly Lijia woman's father had been a wealthy landowner who believed in educating his children, including his daughters. She became the only girl among her peers in the village to attend primary school in the 1930s.

Nowadays, young Lijia couples believe in treating sons and daughters equally. Several villagers, however, mentioned a couple who treated their boy more favorably than their girl, a practice that was severely criticized by other villagers. In the late 1990s, when their first daughter was six years old, the couple had boy-girl twins. According to villagers whom I interviewed, after the couple brought the twins home from the hospital during a cold winter, they placed the boy on the better heated side of the bed and left the girl on the less heated side.[5] The boy became seriously ill when the bed accidentally overheated. Unfortunately, despite medical treatment in the hospital, the newborn boy died. A few villagers criticized the couple for having "black hearts" (*heixin*), meaning evil minds, because they had treated the twins differently. I never discussed the deceased son with the couple to confirm the cause of death because I did not want to inquire about the death of a beloved child unless the couple brought it up. The harsh criticism from villagers, however, reveals that they severely disapprove of gender-biased treatment of children.

This belief in equal treatment of children is also practiced among the majority of young Lijia parents from the time of the conception of a child until the child reaches adulthood. I have never heard of any case of female infant abandonment or infanticide in Lijia Village since the enforcement of the birth-planning policy. I was told about the abortion of female fetuses, although I did not know the names of the particular couples except for one man who confessed to me that his wife aborted a female fetus in order to have a son. As shown in chapter 1, the relatively balanced sex ratio at birth in the township in recent years suggests that sex-selective abortion was not as widely practiced as it was in some regions in China. During my interviews, I even encountered a few women who insisted, against the will of their husbands and parents-in-law, on giving birth to a daughter after an ultrasound revealed a female fetus.

After the birth of a girl, Lijia parents do not stint on a daughter's everyday consumption and medical care, showing love and affection toward a daughter, whom some villagers referred to as "a pearl in the palm" (*zhangshang mingzhu*). Gender does not influence the amount of food, clothing, and toys that a child receives, nor does it determine young parents' decisions on a child's medical treatment. Lijia parents frequently told me stories of caring for a sick daughter. A young Lijia mother, whose infant daughter had a life-threatening illness, spent a sizable amount of money on medical treatments for her daughter, despite her mother-in-law's disapproval of her exhausting family resources to save a girl's life.

This gender-neutral treatment is particularly apparent in parents' commitment to a daughter's education. The decision to support a child's studies is mainly based on how the child performs academically and how motivated the child is to continue with education rather than the child's gender.[6] Lijia parents with a singleton daughter all planned to support her education and offered their daughter opportunities similar to those enjoyed by urban Chinese daughters (Fong 2002; Tsui and Rich 2002). Young parents with more than one child, including at least one daughter, also told me that they would support their children's education equally as long as the children were willing to continue. Among families in which the daughter was more than ten years older than the son, the spacing between the two children gave the parents time to make enough money to support the younger child after focusing financial resources on the older one. During my fieldwork, I have never heard of any case in recent years in which a couple chose to discontinue their support for a promising daughter and only focus family resources on a son.[7]

The belief that parents should support a daughter's education is evident in the villagers' response to a Lijia father's decision to stop supporting his singleton daughter's studies. When Wang Yun, the man's nineteen-year-old daughter, was five years old, her mother died. Despite her being a top student in her class, she dropped out of school in eighth grade because her father was unwilling to continue supporting her. During my interview with her father, he explained that as an outstanding student Wang Yun had a great chance to be admitted by the top senior high school in the county and later by a college. Unfortunately, he did not have the financial resources to pay for a college education for his daughter, nor did he believe that as a single father he could earn enough money through hard work. He thought it was better to stop Wang Yun from advancing to high school. His decision was severely criticized by other villagers, who considered it unwise and nearsighted to withdraw support for an academically high-achieving daughter. One villager told me that if Wang Yun's father had supported her through hard work, she very likely would have gone to college, secured a good-paying job, and been able to support her father in his old age.

One Lijia father who was unable to support one of his daughters for a college education because of financial constraints expressed a deep sense of guilt. In 1995, when his older daughter was preparing to apply to senior high school, his second daughter, who was five years younger, was in primary school. Both daughters were top students and had great potential to go to college. Because of limited family resources, however, he and his wife were well aware that they would not be able to help both daughters attend college. They persuaded their older daughter to give the opportunity for a college education, as a senior sibling's sacrifice, to her younger sister. As a result, although their older daughter's entrance examination score for the top senior high school turned out to be among the highest in her class, she applied to a vocational school that trains school teachers because it was more affordable and because teaching was considered a secure and suitable profession for women. During my interview with the father, he said: "The night before my older daughter left for her vocational school, it was still hard for her to accept the reality that she would not have the opportunity to go to college. My daughter cried and told me: 'In three years when my classmates, who are admitted to the senior high school with much lower scores than mine, go to college, you will regret your decision.'" With tears in his eyes, he said: "I still clearly remember her words. This is my deepest guilt for my daughter." When his older daughter graduated from the vocational school, he helped find her a position in the township middle school where he worked as a Chinese teacher. His daughter was later transferred to a middle school in the county seat after marrying a man whose father was a high-ranking county official. In 2007 the older daughter was living in the county seat with her husband and their son. Despite the daughter's secure job and much improved living conditions, the father still felt guilty for depriving his older daughter of the opportunity to go to college.

Parental support for a daughter's education goes beyond financial provisions. Because of the commonly shared belief that daughters are more delicate and sensitive, Lijia parents make extra efforts to provide care and protection for their daughters. For a daughter in middle school, parents were often actively involved in her daily care, preparing meals, picking her up after school in the evening, and keeping her company late at night while she was working on her schoolwork. During a daughter's senior year in high school, several parents moved near the school to take better care of their daughter.

In the patrilineal Chinese tradition, mothers often took on the role of affectionate nurturers, whereas fathers were stern disciplinarians who remained strict and distant (Ho 1987). An "affectional distance" (Ho 1987, 235) marked the father-child relationship in the Chinese family.[8] In contemporary China, young fathers have developed a strong desire to be more emotionally involved with their children (Jankowiak 2002, 2011; Jankowiak and Moore 2017). Lijia fathers were more open to expressing their affection to a small daughter through touch by holding hands or hugging. Fathers with an older daughter tended to articulate their sentiment in a more reserved way. They expressed love through their daily expenditures on their daughter, as well as in their encouragement and support of her educational attainment. The story of the father's feeling guilty over his inability to support his daughter's college education exemplifies the sense of parental responsibility and love. Another father told how he indulged his eighteen-year-old singleton daughter by allowing her to have as many snacks as she wanted from their family-owned store in the village. "When my daughter was small, we were very poor," he explained. "One day my daughter asked for money for an ice cream bar when a vendor came to the village. We couldn't afford it, and my daughter cried so hard. I felt so bad. We have some money now and can spoil her."

## Conclusion

Young Lijia couples have high expectations for their children's success in adult life and hope that their children can escape the fate of being a peasant and will instead have a financially secure and respectable life in an urban area. While parental desire for a child's success is strong, the increasing cost of a child's daily consumption, driven by rising consumerism and children's demand for consumer goods, has exacerbated the financial burden of childrearing. Raising a successful child also requires parental support for the child's education, another major cost of childrearing. Consequently, an increasing number of young couples have made the decision to have only one child so that they can focus "all resources on only one child" (*ke yige haizi peiyang*), as many parents put it. These young parents have started attending to the quality of their childrearing rather than the number of children they have.

Along with the new preference for having only one child, gendered childrearing practices have also undergone significant transformations. As young couples believe that a daughter can be as successful as a son in educational attainment and career development, they hold a gender-neutral view on the treatments of sons and daughters as well. These parents have been willing to lavish their love and affection on a daughter and offer their wholehearted support for her daily needs and educational pursuits. Gender-neutral parental support and close parent-daughter ties have further encouraged young parents to be satisfied with a singleton daughter and to support her in an unprecedented manner.

# 4

## "Little Quilted Vests to Warm Parents' Hearts"
### Gendered Transformation of Filial Piety

ONE LATE EVENING IN 2005, a Lijia couple in their fifties were forced by their daughter-in-law to move out of their own house, which they shared with their newly married son and his wife. Ever since the young couple's wedding in 2004, the daughter-in-law failed to get along with the elderly couple. The tension intensified one day when the daughter-in-law expressed strong resentment because her mother-in-law had not opened the gate and prepared a meal for her when she returned from herding cattle. The conflict escalated when the daughter-in-law's mother, another Lijia resident, came and supported her daughter in a physical confrontation in which the mother-in-law suffered minor injuries. Immediately following the confrontation, the daughter-in-law declared that the elderly couple had to move out. Otherwise, she would ask for a divorce from their son. To avoid putting their son in a difficult situation, the elderly couple moved out around ten o'clock at night and stayed temporarily with one of the wife's brothers in the village.

When I interviewed the mother-in-law in 2007, she and her husband were living in a small shabby room, next to a livestock room at the brick kiln outside the village, where they worked during the day and served as janitors at night. She told me the story of her attempts to have a daughter during the late 1970s after having given birth to three sons. While pregnant with her fourth child, she had to hide in her relatives' houses in neighboring villages a few times to avoid confrontation with birth-planning officials who tried to persuade her to have an abortion. To her disappointment, she ended up with four sons. For the following twenty years, she and her husband worked exceedingly hard to pay for all their sons' wedding expenses. When they finally financed a wedding for their youngest son, they did not receive anything in return for their efforts; instead, they ended up homeless. The mother told me: "I always wanted a daughter because a daughter is close to her mother's heart. I did not have any luck. If I had a daughter, my life would be much better!" All the elderly parents who told me this couple's story condemned the extremely disrespectful behavior of the daughter-in-law and the cowardice of the son. Some of them also mentioned that if the couple had a daughter, she would certainly offer them support and emotional comfort.

Although the elderly mother's desire for a daughter was never fulfilled, she was pleased to welcome granddaughters into her family. In 2007, among her four married sons, three had a child, and, coincidentally, all were singleton daughters. Strikingly, none of the three sons and daughters-in-law wanted to have a second child, and they all applied for a one-child certificate. When I talked in 2007 to the oldest daughter-in-law, whose daughter was eleven years old, she explained her decision to have a singleton daughter and thus give up the opportunity to have a son: "It is no use having a son. My parents-in-law have four sons. But none of their sons is financially supporting them. They were even kicked out of their own house at night [by the youngest daughter-in-law]. You can't rely on sons to take care of you when you get old."

The story of this Lijia family reveals three major transformations in family dynamics in the village. First, it demonstrates intergenerational conflicts between an elderly couple and a young couple, and the decline of the filial piety of sons and daughters-in-law. Considered a core virtue of family life and a key standard of moral conduct in China, filial piety (*xiao*) refers to serving parents with respect and appreciation, providing them with care and financial support, and practicing ancestor worship after their deaths. The enduring practice of filial piety is still highly valued, especially in rural areas, where the lack of a social security system leaves the majority of elderly peasants with no choice but to rely on their children, especially their sons and daughters-in-law, for support in old age. As has also been documented elsewhere in rural China, despite the cultural significance and financial necessity of filial support, the practice of filial piety among sons has been significantly eroded (Yan 2003; Danyu Wang 2004; Hong Zhang 2004).

Second, the remarks of the elderly mother and the villagers suggest that elderly parents have desired and highly valued an intimate bond with a daughter. The value placed on and appreciation of married daughters reveal a radical shift in view of deeply rooted Confucian ethics and a patrilineal tradition that defined filial piety as a virtue reserved for sons (Knapp 2005; Lo 2004; Tan 2004). In practice, a son was traditionally responsible for offering both financial support and physical care to his parents, for arranging their funerals, and for practicing ancestor worship after their deaths (Baker 1979; Freedman 1970; Hsu 1948). By contrast, a daughter joined her husband's patrilineal family upon marriage and thus was no longer considered a formal member of her natal family. Consequently, she was not expected to make a contribution to her natal family because her filial obligation was transferred to her parents-in-law (R. S. Watson 2004; Wolf and Huang 1980).[1] In contemporary Lijia Village, the role of a daughter in providing emotional and physical support has thus transformed the gendered practice of filial piety.

Third, the story also reveals the impact that the decline of old-age support provided by sons and daughters-in-law has had on the decision among young couples concerning whether to have a second child. The role of adult sons in providing support to parents in old age has been a significant factor contributing to a strong preference for sons in the patrilineal Chinese tradition. The practice is vividly expressed in the well-known Chinese saying, *yang'er fanglao* (raise a son for old-age security). As the oldest daughter-in-law remarked, young Lijia parents have witnessed the weakening of filial support from sons. This transformation of intergenerational exchange has significantly contributed to young couples' decision to forgo the opportunity to have a son and to willingly accept a singleton daughter.

This chapter discusses the gendered transformation of filial piety and its impact on the choice to have a singleton daughter. After examining the arrangements of old-age support in Lijia Village, the chapter explores the decline of financial, physical, and emotional support from sons and daughters-in-law. The discussion then turns to the role of married daughters in providing support to their natal parents. Parents' appreciation of a close bond with a married daughter has led to a reversal of opinion regarding the gendered practice of filial piety, in which daughters are now considered to be more filial. The sociocultural underpinnings of the transformation of the gendered practice of filial piety—a reinterpreted logic of intergenerational exchange, young women's empowerment in marriage and their emerging practice of filial support to their parents, and a shift of postmarital residence and women's socially constructed role as being more considerate than men—are also examined. The chapter concludes with a discussion of the impact of the transformation of filial support on reproductive choice.

## Arrangements for Old-Age Support

Although an extended patrilineal family of three or more generations living under one roof has been the ideal living arrangement among Chinese families, most elderly Lijia parents prefer to postpone dependence on their children for financial support and physical care for as long as they are able. Like the elderly villagers who chose to live alone in rural Hubei (Hong Zhang 2004), elderly Lijia parents prefer to live independently because it not only allows them freedom in such daily activities as choosing their meals and making decisions on budgets but also avoids potential conflicts with their sons and daughters-in-law. As I will discuss later, however, this preference is mainly a response to the decline of financial and physical support and a lack of consideration and respect from adult children, sons and daughters-in-law in particular.

The majority of elderly Lijia residents support themselves financially by farming well into their late sixties or even early seventies. Because of the mechanization of farming, some farm work—plowing, sowing, threshing corn kernels—is performed by machines. In addition, during farming seasons, temporary paid labor, usually offered by women from the village, is widely available. Elderly villagers can either receive assistance from their adult children or hire other villagers for help. When they stop farming, usually when their health significantly declines, they can lease their land for income, in most cases to one of their sons. In 2006, income from renting two people's share of land was 1,110 yuan on average, which provided money for very basic food purchases, such as rice, wheat flour, and cooking oil.

In addition to farming, some elderly men also take temporary employment for extra income. Unlike young villagers who work in factories, in the service industry, and at construction sites, older men in their sixties take less labor-intensive jobs, such as working as a janitor in a factory. Some elderly villagers herd cattle or raise pigs for extra income. Income from farming and other sources is supplemented by gift money from adult children on birthdays and holidays, and among some elderly villagers by occasional support from relatives living in the city. Although the total income does not cover all living expenses, it is sufficient for basic food expenses.

Among elderly parents with severe chronicle health issues or terminal illnesses medical care becomes a significant financial burden.[2] Although the Chinese state has implemented the rural cooperative medical system, which covers a portion of medical care for enrolled rural residents, treatments for severe illness can leave considerable debts not covered by insurance payments.[3] When elderly parents are unable to afford treatments, the child with whom the elderly parent is living is expected to shoulder the financial responsibility. If the cost is exorbitant, all children are expected to share the cost. However, because of the high medical costs, many Lijia families choose not to pay for treatments and instead spend their money on basic care to sustain the elderly parent's life.

Not only do elderly parents make an effort to be financially self-sufficient, they also try to postpone their reliance on their children for physical support. When the health condition of one spouse declines, usually the other spouse becomes the primary care provider and takes daily responsibility for cooking and other household chores. Some adult children help with household chores during their visits, such as washing large pieces of laundry and making bedding. When both spouses become frail and have difficulty performing daily chores, they usually live with the family of one son, and the son's family becomes their care providers. Lijia villagers call this practice *guigei erzi*. The son farms his parents' land, provides financial support and nursing care, arranges his

**Figure 4.** An elderly couple sharing a yard with their only son's family, 2006. The elderly couple lived in the older house (on the right) built in the 1990s and the young couple lived with their daughter in the newer house built in the early 2000s. Note the two piles of corn in the yard. It reveals that the elderly couple and the young couple had separate finances. Each couple stored corn they harvested from their land and would keep the income from selling corn separately.

parents' funerals, and inherits their house and the right to continue to farm their land upon their deaths. Among families with more than one son, the majority of elderly parents follow the customary practice of living with the family of the youngest son because of the practice of serial family division, in which older sons leave their parents' household and establish their independent nuclear households after marriage (Cohen 1992; Yan 2003, 147).

Table 5 reveals the living arrangements and sources of financial support of all elderly Lijia parents who had at least one married child in 2006. As indicated in the table, forty of the eighty-nine couples and widowed or divorced parents were living alone and were financially self-sufficient. These parents farmed their land, and some couples, especially those in their forties, fifties, and sixties, also earned extra income through temporary employment. Six couples and widowed or divorced parents lived alone in a separate house from their children but were financially supported by their children. The child who provided support farmed the parents' land and offered money for food and other expenses. Among the thirteen families in which elderly parents lived with a son's family and were financially self-supporting, the elderly parents had meals with the son's family but had separate finances (a practice called *lianhuo buliancai*). Among the remaining thirty families, elderly parents lived with a son's family and having common finances (a practice called *lianhuo liancai*). It is important to note that among the thirty-six families, in which, elderly parents were either supported by children or had common finances with a son's family, eleven elderly parents and widowed or divorced parents assisted the family financially by herding cattle, for instance, or by taking temporary jobs. In the remaining twenty-five families, the elderly parents were no longer engaged in physical labor because of old age.

**Figure 5.** An elderly couple sharing a house with their youngest son's family, 2006. The elderly couple lived in the room on the left and the young couple lived with their son in the two rooms on the right. Note that there was only one pile of corn in the yard. It reveals that the elderly couple and the young couple had a joint budget.

**Table 5** Living arrangements and sources of financial support for the elderly in Lijia Village, 2006

| Age group | Living alone and self-supporting | Living alone and supported by children | Living with a son's family and self-supporting | Living with a son's family and having common finances |
|---|---|---|---|---|
| Couples 40–49 | 4 | | 1 | 1 |
| Couples 50–59 | 19 | | 7 | 4 |
| Couples 60–69 | 9 | | 2 | 4 |
| Couples 70–79 | 2 | 2 | | 7 |
| Couples over 80 | | | | |
| Women 40–49 | | | | |
| Women 50–59 | 1 | 1 | | 1 |
| Women 60–69 | 1 | 1* | 2 | 5 |
| Women 70–79 | 1 | 1 | | 3* |
| Women over 80 | | | | 1 |
| Men 40–49 | | | | |
| Men 50–59 | 1 | | | |
| Men 60–69 | 2 | | | 1 |
| Men 70–79 | | 1 | 1 | 1 |
| Men over 80 | | | | 2 |
| Total | 40 | 6 | 13 | 30 |

*The woman (60–69) and one of the women (70–79) were supported by a daughter and a son-in-law.

An arrangement between an elderly Lijia couple and their four sons and one daughter exemplifies the practice of elderly support in Lijia Village. In 2007, they were in their late seventies. Except for their third son and their daughter their children lived in the village. The elderly couple supported themselves financially by leasing their land to their youngest son. They also received gift money for their birthdays and on holidays from all their children except for the oldest son and daughter-in-law as a result of the mother-in-law's long-term conflict with the daughter-in-law. Five years before, when the elderly parents needed help paying for digging a well inside their yard, the elderly father's brother from the city offered to make a contribution and initiated talks with their sons for sharing the rest of the cost. In the summer of 2010, when I visited the couple, the elderly father, who used to be a sharp-minded man, was showing signs of dementia. Needing support, the couple moved in with their youngest son's family in 2011.

## Sons as Unreliable Providers

Arrangements for elderly support are seldom made without disagreements among multiple sons and frustration and disappointment from elderly parents. Although elderly parents feel entitled to receive support from their children, especially from those who farm their land, adult children often disagree on their shared responsibilities, including paying for a parent's medical expenses, and entitled rights, including the right to inherit their parents' house.[4] As a result, some adult children abandon their filial duties. Disputes also occur between adult children and their elderly parents when children believe that their parents have not treated them equally (for instance, helping with childcare for one child but not others or offering a larger amount of money to finance the wedding of one of the sons). In those cases, the children are usually reluctant to fulfill their filial duties. When intergenerational conflicts intensify between elderly parents and the family of one son, usually with a daughter-in-law, the son's family often refuses to provide any support, as is demonstrated in the case in which the oldest son and daughter-in-law abandoned their filial responsibility because of conflicts with the elderly mother.

When all adult children abandon their filial duties, elderly parents have no choice but to turn to the village head or a respected family relative or friend who can serve as a mediator. When mediation fails, elderly parents can file a lawsuit against their children. Because the laws in China stipulate that adult children have the responsibility to provide support for parents in need, the court usually supports elderly parents in such lawsuits.[5] Taking legal recourse, however, is considered a last resort because bringing a family dispute to court is considered extremely disgraceful and could severely hurt the relationship with adult children. In recent years, three elderly Lijia parents sued their adult children for financial support. In one case, an elderly father filed a lawsuit against his four sons because they refused to pay for his medical treatments. After the court went to the village to investigate his case, he changed his mind and asked to withdraw the lawsuit. The court required that each son pay fifty yuan to share a fee of two hundred yuan for withdrawing the lawsuit. A year after the elderly man's death, his wife explained to me that they had been worried that the lawsuit would offend their sons and that none of their sons would be willing to arrange the funeral and pay for the expenses when the father died. When the father passed away, his sons arranged a funeral for him.

In another case, an elderly widow, out of desperation and at the urging of one of her daughters-in-law, sought a ruling from the court for support from her five sons. Her five sons failed to reach an agreement on their shared responsibilities for supporting her. The youngest daughter-in-law, with whom the elderly mother was living, verbally abused her and even smashed a window in her room, out of frustration because the responsibility of caring for her mother-in-law had been left to the youngest couple. The elderly mother eventually filed a lawsuit against her five sons. The court demanded that her five sons rotate the responsibility of providing meals for the elderly mother. When I interviewed the elderly woman in 2007, she confessed to me that she really had no choice but to sue her five sons. She sadly commented that, even though she was offered enough food, her relationship with her five sons and daughters-in-law had not improved because the lawsuit had obviously hurt their feelings.

In addition to a decline in financial support and physical care for the elderly, elderly parents often lament a lack of consideration and respect from adult children, especially sons and daughters-in-law. The desire for a close bond with and respect from a child is demonstrated by the responses of thirty-four elderly parents with married sons and daughters to my open-ended question on their definition of filiality.[6] In addition to twelve elderly parents who mentioned offering of financial support (*yanghuo laoren*), providing food (*geifanchi*), helping with work (*bangganhuo*), and offering money (*geiqianhua*) as the most important of their expectations for filial support, twenty-two elderly parents prioritized keeping parents in mind (*dianji*) and visiting parents frequently (*changhuijia kankan*). According to these elderly parents, filial children should regularly check with their parents about their well-being and visit them frequently. Additionally, twenty respondents emphasized not making parents upset (*bure laoren shengqi*), not criticizing them (*buchi'er laoren*), and not subjecting them to physical or verbal abuse (*budani bumani*).

Some elderly parents who were living with a son's family complained about a lack of consideration from the son's family, serving food, for instance, that was hard for elderly people to chew and digest. Some elderly were also disappointed that their children did not express concern for them frequently. One fifty-five-year-old woman complained about her son's lack of expression of loving care: "A couple of weeks ago, my leg hurt and everybody in my family knew about it. My son shares a house with me. But he never asked about my leg after he came back from work in the evening." Not only were elderly parents disappointed about their children's lack of consideration, many parents also lamented a loss of respect from their adult children. Such laments were derived from increasing conflicts with adult children, sons and daughters-in-law in particular. The most extreme cases of disrespect involve verbal abuse and physical violence. My interviews with the thirty-four elderly parents revealed that twenty-three had engaged in at least one intense verbal confrontation with their son or daughter-in-law. Disappointed and even outraged, some of the elderly parents indicated with some irony that they would consider their children filial if their sons and daughters-in-law did not physically or verbally abuse them (*buda buma jiushi xiao*).

Women still take the major responsibility for household chores, such as cooking and doing laundry, and elderly parents who require physical care usually rely on a daughter-in-law for daily support. Elderly women often compare the practice of their daughters-in-law with their own filial practice or that of an earlier generation. They often emphasize the authority that parents used to be able to exert over daughters-in-law and the reverence and submission of the daughter-in-law to their parents-in-law. According to these elderly parents, a daughter-in-law used to serve her in-laws every day, such as preparing water for them to wash their faces in the morning and serving them meals, and would work under their supervision in such matters as performing household chores and childrearing. An elderly woman in her early eighties commented that in her day, "if a mother-in-law said, 'eggs come from trees,' a daughter-in-law did not dare to say no." Elderly parents complain about the decline of parental authority over their married children and the emerging empowerment of daughters-in-law, often quoting the well-circulated saying in the village: "Nowadays, a daughter-in-law behaves like a mother-in-law" (*erxifu chengle laopopo*). When elderly parents do not get along with a daughter-in-law, it can significantly affect the quality of care they receive.

Even when elderly parents make an effort to maintain a good relationship with a daughter-in-law, the delicate nature of the relationship can create emotional stress for them, as is demonstrated by the story of a Lijia widow. A few years after her husband's death, she managed to finance a wedding for her singleton son and lived in the same house with the young couple. According to my interviews with villagers, the woman had no intention of remarrying and planned to live with her son's family for the rest of her life. But her daughter-in-law preferred a private conjugal life and frequently expressed discontent when her husband showed a close bond with his mother by offering an ice cream bar to his mother, for instance, before giving one to her. Eventually, the woman decided to remarry to avoid putting her son in a difficult situation and accepted a marriage proposal from a widower in another village. One villager, the woman's former neighbor, told me that "on the day she left for her new husband's village, she left everything with her son and daughter-in-law [out of love for her son] and only took one wrapped package with her. It was sad to watch."

### Daughters as Filial Supporters

While filial support provided by sons and daughters-in-law has declined, married daughters have nevertheless begun to provide emotional, physical, and even financial support to their parents. The increasing contributions of daughters are widely recognized and greatly valued by their elderly parents.[7] My interviews with the thirty-four elderly Lijia parents with married sons and daughters reveal that elderly couples are more likely to associate filiality with daughters. Among these elderly parents, eighteen (52.9 percent) believed that daughters are more filial. Four (11.8 percent) stated that sons are more filial but did not deny daughters' filiality. The remaining twelve (35.3 percent) acknowledged that sons can be as filial as daughters but only if they can gain their wives' support. Young couples shared similar views. The results of a survey that I conducted with 248 couples under fifty in Lijia Village and a neighboring village demonstrate that although the majority did not associate filial piety with gender, twenty-seven percent believed that daughters are more filial, while only three percent believed that sons demonstrate greater filiality. Elderly parents often express their appreciation for daughters with a well-known Chinese saying: "A daughter is like a little quilted vest to warm her parents' hearts" (*nuer shi diemade tiexin xiaomian'ao*). Vests are a traditional cotton garment that women make for family members against the cold weather during the long winters in Northeast China. Just like a little quilted vest that offers warmth in a cold winter, a daughter shares an intimate bond with her parents, making her close to their hearts.

When describing a daughter's filial devotion to her parents, elderly parents would often use the story of Li Lan, a Lijia daughter who was considered a model of filiality. Li Lan was adopted by an infertile Lijia couple when she was three months old. According to my interviews with Li Lan and other villagers, she was a filial daughter to her adoptive parents, even after she learned about her adoption. At nineteen, she started to earn a salary by working as a village health practitioner. She always bought her adoptive parents their favorite food and, occasionally, nice clothes when she visited the county seat. After she married, although she had the opportunity to live in the county seat where her husband was from, Li Lan chose to live with her adoptive parents so that she could take care of them on a daily basis. Li Lan's adoptive father died in 1990 and, coincidentally, on the very same day, her biological father also passed away.[8] Although she was expected to attend her biological father's funeral, Li Lan decided to stay to arrange a funeral for her adoptive father. Five years later, her adoptive mother suffered a cerebral hemorrhage. Li Lan tried all available means to save her mother's life, including desperately kowtowing on the floor, a traditional way to pray, until her forehead was swollen. Her mother survived the initial crisis. Later, when her mother's illness became more severe and required constant care, including cleaning up her excrement, Li Lan fulfilled her obligation as a caring daughter until her mother's death. Villagers praised Li Lan highly for her extraordinary self-sacrifice and dedication in performing filial piety. One elderly woman was very impressed with Li Lan's devotion to her adopted mother: "She always kept her mother's bedsheet very clean even on the last day of her mother's life." While comparing the filial practice of sons and daughters, some elderly parents mentioned Li Lan's story and commented that "even an adopted daughter is more filial than most sons."

My further exploration of filial support provided by married daughters reveals that a daughter's filiality is first manifested by her emotional and physical support of her parents. A daughter expresses her consideration for and her emotional bond with her parents through her frequent visits. Elderly parents value frequent visits from their married children and some would express this expectation with the title of a popular Chinese song, "Visit Home Often." The song portrays a married couple returning home with their child and gifts. It was first sung on television on a national Chinese New Year celebration in 1999 and soon gained popularity throughout China. An elderly woman told me: "As the song says, it's not important how much money our children give us. We are happy if they can visit us frequently. It's the best way to show that they really care about us." Some elderly parents told me that their daughters would visit with food, such as dumplings, that they had prepared. Some mentioned that they helped with household chores. Others enjoyed chatting with their daughters, who shared stories of their lives and comforted their parents when they were going through emotional distress.

Daughters' frequent visits were relatively easy because most marriages were within the local township. As indicated in Table 6, in 2006 thirty-four of the Lijia daughters (23 percent of the 148 respondents) resided in the village, either through marrying a Lijia man or by moving back to the village after marriage. My interviews with the parents of some of these daughters show that their daughters visited them on a daily basis. The ninety-five daughters (64 percent) who moved into their husbands' village in the same township, the same county, or in a neigh-

**Table 6** Postmarital residence of married daughters from Lijia Village, 2006*

| Postmarital residence of daughters | Number | % |
|---|---|---|
| Residence in Lijia Village | | |
| Married a man from the village | 23 | 15.5 |
| Moved back to the village after marriage | 11 | 7.4 |
| Residence outside Lijia Village | | |
| Residence in the same township | 38 | 25.7 |
| Residence in the same county | 52 | 35.1 |
| Residence in a neighboring county | 5 | 3.4 |
| Residence in the same city | 10 | 6.8 |
| Residence in the same province | 3 | 2.0 |
| Residence outside the province | 6 | 4.1 |
| Total | 148 | 100 |

*The age range of these married daughters was 19 to 55.

boring county, usually lived within a half hour's bus ride of Lijia Village. The proximity and the convenience of local transportation facilitated frequent visits. A seventy-nine-year-old woman who married into Lijia Village from a neighboring village told me that when she was married in the 1940s, there was no bus transportation. A one-way trip to her parents' village took about an hour. Now it took her daughter, who married into the same neighboring village, ten minutes to travel to Lijia Village by bus. The frequent visits of married daughters have become a significant aspect of daughters' filial practice nowadays compared to daughters' visits in the past, when visiting natal parents was subject to the approval of their husbands and parents-in-law and was constrained by a lack of convenient transportation.

In addition to emotional and physical support, some married daughters also provide financial support to their parents when their economic conditions permit.[9] When sons neglect or abandon their filial duty, most married daughters shoulder the responsibility. In a few cases in which elderly parents in need do not receive regular financial support from any of their sons, a daughter would make an effort to provide food and clothes during her frequent visits. A few Lijia daughters even contribute more than the sons do toward their parents' medical care, even though they are not expected to take a larger share of this financial obligation.

## Interpreting the Transformation of the Gendered Practice of Filial Support

The transformation of the gendered practice of filial support and the changing perception of daughters as being more filial presents a significant and fundamental shift in intergenerational relations and patrilineal traditions in rural China. Several factors have contributed to the change: reinterpreted intergenerational relations; young women's empowerment in marriage and their emerging filial practice with their parents; a shift of postmarital residence and women's socially constructed role as being more considerate than men.

The weakening of filial support provided by sons is closely associated with the decline in parental power in rural China, where during the collective period communes replaced family-based farming, which was controlled by an elderly patriarch. In the early years of this period, some young Lijia couples took the initiative in joining a production team, thus gaining independence from their patriarchal families. An eighty-year-old man recalled that when collectivization was first enforced, he and his wife were living with their newly married son and daughter-in-law and five younger unmarried children. When villagers were encouraged to volunteer for a production team, he and his wife were unwilling to join. Their son and daughter-in-law, however, were ready to become two of the first production team members. The young couple then proposed a family division and joined a production team. Although unhappy with the decision, the parents had to accept it because joining a production team was strongly supported by the government and was becoming unavoidable. A series of government-initiated policies beginning in the 1950s, including the abolition of arranged marriage and banning of ancestor worship, had also shaken traditional patriarchal practice (Davis and Harrell 1993; Yan 2003). Patriarchal control was further weakened after the introduction of the market economy in the early 1980s, allowing young couples to achieve economic independence through nonagricultural employment.

With the loss of patriarchal authority, intergenerational relations had to be renegotiated and reinterpreted (Croll 2006b; Yuhua Guo 2001; Yan 2003). For the young generation, unconditional filial devotion has been replaced by a sense of intergenerational reciprocity: a child's filiality must be earned through the parents fulfilling their role as loving providers for the child's education and career development, and, most of all, in financing a son's wedding. After a son's wedding, parents must cultivate and maintain good relations with their married sons and daughters-in-law, with appropriate help with childcare and household chores, for instance, when young couples are in need. Under the reinterpreted intergenerational relations, young married women tend to expect substantial bridewealth and continuous assistance from their parents-in-law (see chapter 5). Therefore, when a daughter-in-law is not provided with appropriate bridewealth or believes that her in-laws have not offered enough help, she is likely to be reluctant to assist her husband in fulfilling his filial obligations. Dissatisfaction with her parents-in-law can often result in disrespectful behavior and, ultimately, a negative influence on the husband's filial practice toward his parents.

Meanwhile, these young women have little expectation of a high dowry from their parents, because the groom's family is expected to shoulder the major responsibility of financing a wedding. Further, many parents play an important role in helping a daughter's family—by lending them money or babysitting their grandchildren—even though they are not expected to make a contribution. Their help is usually interpreted as an expression of love for their daughters and is always greatly appreciated by their daughters and sons-in-law. Consequently, there are fewer conflicts between a married daughter and her parents over parental obligations. A harmonious relationship facilitates the daughter's filial practice toward her parents.

While the reinterpreted intergenerational relations have weakened the institutionalized practice of old-age support by sons, young women's income-earning power and their decision-making leverage in marriage have enabled them to offer filial support to their natal parents. As discussed in chapter 2, a large number of married women earn an income by engaging in nonagricultural employment. The money they bring home has become an important source of family income. Women who do not take nonagricultural employment shoulder the responsibility for farm work while their husbands work outside the village. Men value their wives' economic contribution as well as their work at home. A man in his mid-forties frankly confessed: "I went to the city to work in a factory last year. My wife did all the farm work at home. After we calculated our income, I was surprised to find that she made more money by farming than I did by working in the factory. She is truly a capable and hard worker." With their income-earning power women can use family resources for their natal parents. They are able to offer their parents money or gifts on certain occasions as well as participate in reciprocity with their natal relatives. During my fieldwork, I was surprised to find that some women even put a portion of their income into a personal fund instead of pooling the money in a joint fund with their husband's income and would spend some of the money in their personal savings on their natal family. Further, having gained an upper hand in marriage in a sex-ratio imbalanced marriage market, young women are able to make their own decisions regarding filiality toward parents (see chapter 5 for further discussion).

Married men whom I interviewed recognized women's emerging empowerment, and some quoted a version of Chairman Mao's famous slogan of gender equality, "Women hold up half the sky," which they have modified to "Women can hold up more than half the sky" (*nüren nengding duobanbiantian*). The recognition of women's increased status has had a direct influence on men's filial practice. Some married men told me that they would like to fulfill their filial obligation to their parents, but if it should cause a problem for their wives, they would compromise so as to maintain marital harmony. The story of a thirty-seven-year-old Lijia man provides an example. He told me in 2004 that early that year his wife decided to offer a gift of a hundred yuan for her father's birthday, but he proposed fifty yuan instead. His wife argued: "My parents raised me for over twenty years. Now I am married to you and have borne children for your family. My parents got nothing for raising me. Why should it be a problem to give them just a hundred yuan!" His wife's remarks rendered him speechless, and he reluctantly agreed to the amount of money his wife wanted.

Some young married men even made an effort to gain favor with their parents-in-law to please their wives. Almost all the men I interviewed said that they offer money and gifts to their parents-in-law on birthdays and holidays. Many help them with farm work, house construction, and family events. In some cases, as the following story demonstrates, young married men even compete with each other to win favor from their parents-in-law. In 2007, I attended the wedding of a young couple. While enjoying a joyful ceremony with a large turnout of guests, I was surprised to find that one of the groom's two brothers-in-law had invited ten friends to the wedding. This behavior made the other brother-in-law very upset. When I talked to one of the groom's cousins, a twenty-seven-year-old married man, he explained that the brother-in-law brought his friends to the wedding to please his parents-in-law because a large attendance indicates the parents-in-law's popularity. The other brother-in-law was jealous and upset because he had just lost the rivalry over gaining favor with his parents-in-law. Many elderly people severely criticized the emerging practice of married men's favoring their parents-in-law to please their wives, frequently citing a popular saying in the village: "Marrying in a daughter-in-law is equal to marrying off a son" (*quge xifu guochuquge erzi*). In these cases, China's long-standing tradition of a married woman's contributing to her husband's filial practice has been reversed to a man's helping his wife to practice filial piety to her parents.

Finally, shifts in postmarital residence from patrilocal to neolocal and in women's socially constructed role to being more considerate than men have further contributed to the belief of a daughter's filiality. Elders who have been left with an empty nest are found to be more likely to feel lonely (Yang and Victor 2008). As is shown in table 6, forty-six (51.7 percent) elderly parents lived alone in 2006. My interviews with these parents reveal that they especially had a desire for frequent visits from their children. The shift of postmarital residence has relieved married women from the daily responsibility of taking care of their parents-in-law. They can decide to whom they prefer to perform filiality and are more willing to follow their hearts and show their attachment to their parents. Children's filial practice is often motivated by a sense of guilt and gratitude toward parents (Evans 2008; Fong 2004). A thirty-eight-year-old woman told me: "During the years when I went to school, my mother got up early every morning to cook me breakfast. Whenever I recall this, I cannot help but feel like doing something for my mother to pay back everything she has done for me."

Villagers attribute their daughters' consideration to a socially constructed notion of women as being, by nature, more caring and more likely to express their feelings than men. Women are believed to have warm hearts (*xinchangre*) and to be more sensitive (*xinxi*) to parents' practical and emotional needs. When a conflict arises between an elderly couple and their married sons and daughters-in-law, a daughter is a valuable source of comfort and support. Sons, on the contrary, are considered insensitive (*xincu*) by nature and less likely to show emotional intimacy toward their parents. The majority of men whom I interviewed shared the same view. Some claimed that they wanted to show intimacy toward their parents but felt shy about expressing their emotions for fear of leaving the impression of being womanlike. A married man explained to me that he did not talk to his parents as much as a daughter would because as the breadwinner of his family, he should show his strong side. "I will appear a weak person if I talk with my parents about my frustrations and worries."

### "If Sons Aren't Filial, It Is No Use Having a Son": Filial Support and Reproductive Choice

The decline in sons' filial support has weakened the desire for a son among young Lijia parents, who often said: "If sons aren't filial, it is no use having a son" (*erzi buxiao, youerzi yemeiyong*). Lijia couples faced with the decision of having a second child are usually the care providers for their aging parents. Not only have these couples witnessed the tension and conflicts between elderly parents and their sons and daughters-in-law, they have even engendered the decline of sons' filial support. Like the oldest daughter-in-law at the beginning of this chapter, some Lijia villagers use their family's experience to explain their choice not to have a second child. In 2006, I interviewed a Lijia couple who were in their thirties and who had a ten-year-old singleton daughter. It took the couple several years to finally reach the decision not to have a second child. In the past, the husband had always wanted a son and was a strong supporter for a second child. The wife, however, was concerned about the burden of raising a second child. She finally decided not to have a second child and persuaded her husband to agree to apply for a one-child certificate in 2005. Explaining her decision, she told me that one of the major contributing factors was sons' failure to offer their parents filial support. This was the case with her own husband and his five brothers and her own brother who treated her parents with disrespect as well. When her husband expressed his disappointment with not having a son, she retorted: "What is the use having a son? Your parents have six sons. But which one of you has supported them?" Her remarks rendered her husband speechless.

Because young Lijia couples can no longer take it for granted that their sons will support them in their old age and also because the majority of these couples have only one child, they have adopted a notion of self-reliance (*kaoziji*)—or "two-handed preparation" (*liangshou zhunbei*)—for self-support in old age in case their children turn out to be unreliable or the burden of elder care becomes too heavy on an only child. One way is to build savings by maximizing family income. Some couples told me that they would work hard to make as much money as possible while they still could. If their child should prove unreliable when they reached old age, as long as they had savings, they could find a way to support themselves and could pay someone to help. A Lijia couple, both of whom held positions at the township government, hired a caretaker for the husband's elderly mother. Some villagers mentioned this arrangement as a possible option.

As a way to prepare for self-support in old age, a large number of young couples had recently bought eldercare insurance (*yanglao baoxian*) from insurance companies. The insurance was set up as old-age security funds, paid for in annual installments for a set period. When the period ended, usually when the insurer reached retirement age, the person could receive payments from the account. Among 212 married Lijia couples below the age of fifty-seven in 2007, ninety-nine couples (46.7 percent) had chosen to purchase at least one insurance policy for one spouse.[10] Sixty-two (62.6 percent) among these ninety-nine couples had purchased one policy for each spouse. Strikingly, sixty-one among the ninety-nine couples (61.6 percent) who had purchased at least one policy had a son.

In addition to preparing for self-support, couples who had a daughter made an effort to offer her the best possible upbringing and cultivate a close bond with her.[11] A few Lijia parents who had a singleton daughter mentioned that "raising a filial daughter is more important than trying to have a son who may turn out to be unfilial." Close ties with daughters were maintained after her marriage. Some parents whose married daughter lived in the village had offered to help a daughter with childcare. Others spent significant time with a daughter when she visited. While keeping a close bond with a daughter came out of parental love and affection, the parents also expected that the bond would be sustained through their old age and that their daughter would be reliable when they needed support.

### Conclusion

The practice of old-age support has undergone major transformations as filial support from sons and daughters-in-law has declined. Meanwhile, married daughters have started to provide physical, emotional, and even financial support to their parents and have proven to be more filial than married sons. Aging parents recognize and show appreciation for a daughter's filiality. The transformation is the result of a reinterpreted logic of intergenerational exchange. In addition, women's emerging empowerment in marriage and engagement in employment enable them to make decisions that affect their ability to practice filiality. Finally, a shift of postmarital residence from patrilocal to neolocal has contributed to the elderly's increasing desire to maintain emotional bonds, and women's socially constructed role makes them more likely to meet elderly parents' expectations.

This gendered shift in filial support is one of the decisive factors contributing to a decline of son preference in reproductive choice. Young Lijia couples have not only witnessed the gendered transformation of filial support, they have engendered it. As they have come to realize that having a son no longer guarantees a secure old age and that aging parents can rely on a daughter, these couples have willingly embraced a singleton daughter. Along with making their own arrangements to provide for their old age, they have made an effort to cultivate and maintain a close bond with a daughter.

# 5

## "Here Comes My Big Debt"
### Wedding Costs and Sons as Financial Burdens

IN 2006, a young woman named Liu Hong was awaiting the birth of her first child. She expressed to me her excitement and anxiety about the upcoming birth. Disclosure of the sex of a fetus during ultrasound examinations was prohibited, so Liu Hong did not know whether her baby was a boy or a girl. She had mixed feelings about her expectations: "The ideal is a boy and a girl. But it costs too much to pay for a son's wedding. And you have to serve (*cihou*) him even after he gets married. It is better to have only a girl. If the child is a boy, we will have to work for him for the rest of our lives. . . . In the past, everyone wanted to have sons (*pan erzi*). Nowadays, people have a fear of sons (*pa erzi*)."

Two days later, Liu Hong gave birth to a healthy boy at the hospital in the county seat. She asked me to give her son a name because she considered me well educated and trusted that I would be able to recommend a nice name for her son. After spending a couple of hours flipping through a Chinese dictionary, I came up with a list of ten names for a boy. When I called her the next morning to explain the meaning behind each of the names, she stopped me after the first name, Shuhan, a name with the two Chinese characters for "book" and "being well cultivated." "This is it!" Liu Hong said firmly, "I want my son to be well educated." I was not at all surprised by her choice because I had heard many young parents tell me repeatedly of having the same expectations for their children's educational achievements. Not long after expressing her aspiration for her son's education, however, Liu Hong started to feel the pressure of the unavoidable obligation to finance her son's wedding. When I visited her in the hospital, she was recovering from the cesarean delivery. After responding to my inquiry about her recovery, she looked at her newborn son and said: "Here comes my big debt [*dajihuang laile*]!"[1]

The story of Liu Hong reveals the heavy parental obligation to finance a son's wedding and the anxiety and pressure thereby imposed on young couples who have a son. While the role of sons as care providers for aging parents has significantly changed, the escalating cost of financing a wedding has turned sons into financial burdens. This chapter explores the ways in which the exorbitant cost of weddings and the unavoidable parental obligation to finance a son's wedding have contributed to the weakening of the desire for a son among young Lijia couples. First, the significant increase in the cost of a son's wedding in recent years is discussed in relation to young women's agency in demanding an expensive wedding in the sex-ratio imbalanced marriage market. The chapter then turns to parental obligations and the long-term preparations for a son's wedding. In addition to providing financial support for a son's wedding, Lijia parents are expected to continue their support for a son's family after his marriage. The chapter concludes with an examination of the impact of the heavy parental responsibility for a son on a couple's choosing to have only a singleton daughter.

## The Skyrocketing Cost of a Wedding

Although singleness can be associated with an independent lifestyle among the elite and the middle-class in urban and cosmopolitan settings, for the majority of Chinese people, marriage has been considered not a personal choice but an indispensable life stage for both men and women (Attané et al. 2013; Liu 2000, 75; Ownby 2002; Oxfeld 2010, 105). Marriage is especially crucial for men because a man is expected to have at least one child through marriage to continue his patrilineal family line (Ownby 2002). Further, the gender division of labor in the household relegates to woman the major responsibility of household chores and caregiving for children and for elderly parents. A Lijia bachelor spoke of a man's desiring a wife for companionship and comfortable living conditions. While his sister-in-law commented that without a family that demands support, a bachelor is burden free, the forty-six-year-old divorced man disagreed: "But it is still better to be married. A married man has a hot meal and a heated bed ready when he comes home from work. Without a wife, a man has to heat the bed and prepare a meal on his own." More important, getting married is a critical rite of passage that establishes a man's status in his community (Ownby 2002; J. Watson 2004). For example, in rural Hong Kong, having a marriage name granted a man the status of adulthood and the right to participate in lineage and community rituals (R. S. Watson 1986).

Bachelorhood in China is an extremely marginalized social category, associated with disgrace and failure in life (Han 2009; J. Watson 2004). The stigma attached to bachelorhood is demonstrated by a conversation that I had with a Lijia family at a dinner in 2006. A middle-aged man who had remained a bachelor until he married a widow in his late thirties remarked: "A man has to get married. He needs a wife to take care of the house." His brother-in-law, a widower, offered a different perspective: "That is not the point of marriage! If you are a bachelor, people don't treat you as a human being!" Shocked, I asked why bachelors were treated differently. The two men remained silent. The elderly mother then answered: "People don't treat bachelors seriously. They say, 'What is the point of talking with a bachelor?'" Her remarks reminded me of several occasions when I had mentioned to my female research assistant and my friends in the village that I intended to interview several bachelors. They strongly recommended that I not do this, and all for the same reason—they felt that bachelors do not have anything valuable to say. Villagers consider bachelors losers because they are deemed either not good enough for marriage or too lazy to earn enough money to finance a wedding. My in-depth interviews on this matter revealed, however, that bachelorhood is more a result of family poverty than the man's personal character.[2] Additionally, married men are often antagonistic toward bachelors, considering them potential seducers of married women and thus threats to their marriage. Thus, the fear of being an outcast in their community and the yearning for love and companionship drive rural men to try any means possible to find a marriage partner. While men have a strong desire to marry, the expectation that groom's family will finance his wedding creates tremendous pressure for a young man and his family during his search for a wife. Although bridewealth and dowries coexist in Chinese traditions (Croll 1981; Murphy 2001; Siu 1993), the groom's family is expected to shoulder the lion's share of wedding expenses (Oxfeld 2010; Parish and Whyte 1978; Sargeson 2004; Yan 2003). With the skyrocketing expense of weddings since the 1990s, this enduring tradition has been increasingly skewed to the disadvantage of the groom's family (Fong 2004; Sargeson 2004; Yan 2003). While any financial contribution from the bride's family is counted as a goodwill gesture, the pressure for the groom's family to fulfill their obligation to pay for wedding expenses has trapped many rural families in severe debt.

In Lijia Village, the dowry (*peisong*) is the contribution of the bride's parents to her wedding, which takes the form of money and/ or household items, such as electrical devices, furniture, and bedding items. Compared with the increasing demand for bridewealth, the expectation for a dowry is very limited. In fact, there is no fixed amount for a dowry because the amount is entirely the decision of the bride's parents. The majority of parents, especially those who are well-to-do, try to offer a decent dowry. Impoverished parents, however, can either use a portion of the bridewealth that their daughters have received from the groom's family or use their own money to buy a few household items for the young couple, which then counts as the dowry. Thus, it is easy to meet the obligation to provide a daughter with a dowry. Parents who had married off their daughters between 2004 and 2006 told me that the amount of dowry that they offered ranged from five thousand to ten thousand yuan.

Although a dowry is not demanded, once it is offered, it is considered a goodwill gesture from the bride's parents and is greatly appreciated. Low expectations for a dowry are derived from the traditional belief that, once a daughter is married, she belongs to her husband's family, which benefits from her labor and from any children she produces (Freedman 1966). The daughter's parents raise her without receiving anything in return; thus, raising a daughter for her future husband's family is the parents' greatest contribution. It is thus understandable that, although parents do not offer a dowry, they are still treated with gratitude. In fact, during my fieldwork, to show their appreciation for the bride's parents and respect for the bride, the groom's parents had started to offer an additional gift of ten percent of her dowry.

The average amount of a dowry in 2006 (5,000–10,000 yuan) stood in stark contrast to the average amount expected from the groom's family for a wedding, a hundred thousand yuan, which is an astronomical figure for the majority of Lijia families. The cost can be broken down into six major categories: bridewealth (*ganzhe*), a house, jewelry (*sanjin*), a motorcycle, household items, and an engagement reception and wedding banquet. Bridewealth is the amount of money demanded by the bride and offered by the groom's family. The money is transferred to the bride through an initial payment of several thousand yuan at an engagement reception, with a second payment, usually saved in a bank account in the bride's name, before the wedding. Since the 1980s, the ownership of bridewealth has gradually shifted from the bride's parents to the bride herself.[3] The majority of women I interviewed used their bridewealth for their nuclear family. During the 1980s and the early 1990s, when the majority of young couples did not own a house at the time of their wedding, it was typical for a young couple to spend the bridewealth on a house and establish their own household within a few years after their wedding. Since the late 1990s, when brides began to demand a house as part of the wedding agreement, some women have saved their bridewealth in a bank account or have used it for household expenses, such as a home renovation.

The amount of bridewealth has increased exponentially since the 1990s. According to my research on twenty-eight marriages between 1975 and 2007, the amount has risen from an average of 306 yuan between the mid-1970s and the mid-1980s, to four thousand yuan in the early 1990s, and to 22,154 yuan in the 2000s. The average bridewealth from 2004 to 2007 was 29,600 yuan, more than seventy times the amount of bridewealth thirty years earlier.[4] The drastic increase was well characterized by a fifty-year-old woman in 2007. She was shocked at the large amount that her son's girlfriend requested: "Nowadays young women ask for too much. When I was married, I was given only three hundred yuan. I was not even worth the price you would pay for a pig today!"

While the increasing expenses for bridewealth have become a heavy burden on the groom's family, the obligation to provide a house has further strained wedding financing. As has been documented elsewhere in urban (Fong 2002; Li Zhang 2010; Zhang and Sun 2014) and rural areas (Oxfeld 2010; Sargeson 2004; Siu 1993) in China, providing housing for a young couple has become a requirement for the groom's family during wedding preparations. A newly built or a well-renovated house can be a decisive factor for a marriage proposal. In Lijia Village, many young people rely on a family friend or relative to introduce a match for them. If both parties are satisfied with their initial meetings and willing to proceed, the young woman and her family will be invited to the man's family home. The practice is called seeing the house (*kanjia*)—in other words, inspecting the financial situation and living environment of the potential husband's family. I was told that in several cases the young woman rejected a marriage proposal because a man's parents could not afford to either renovate a house or provide the young woman with money as compensation for a house. Therefore, the son's family must now prepare a well-renovated house before a marriage proposal is offered. A rise in competitive consumption has increased the expectation for housing, thus exacerbating the already heavy burden of wedding financing. Lijia families follow the latest trends in housing renovations, installing heating pipes or building a separate bathroom and an enclosed kitchen. When a house is too old to be renovated, the family must tear it down and build a new one, which is a much greater expense. In 2006, it cost from thirty thousand up to seventy thousand yuan to renovate or to build a house.

In addition to bridewealth and a house, other major items for a wedding in 2006 included three pieces of gold jewelry for the bride, such as a ring, a necklace, a bracelet, and a pair of earrings; a motorcycle; such household items as electronic equipment (see fig. 6), a washing machine, furniture, and bedding. The groom's family is also expected to pay for an engagement dinner and a wedding banquet (see fig. 7). The bride determined the amount for jewelry, and the cost in 2006 ranged between three thousand and five thousand yuan. Because a

**Figure 6.** The groom and the bride's room on the wedding day, 2007.

motorcycle offered convenient transportation to the county seat and areas where temporary jobs were available and for visiting family and relatives, a motorcycle was a frequent demand during negotiations. If a family did not own a motorcycle at the time of a marriage proposal, it would
cost about five thousand yuan to buy a new one in 2006. The expenses
for electronics, furniture, other living necessities, an engagement dinner,

**Figure 7.** A wedding banquet, 2007. The groom's parents hired a chef and his team to prepare the banquet. The guests are enjoying a meal inside a tent set up in the yard outside the house of the groom's parents.

and a wedding banquet could add up to at least another twenty thousand yuan.

The wedding expenses for the groom's family can thus amount to about a hundred thousand yuan. The amount has been increasing with the escalating price of bridewealth and as new consumer goods (such as a desktop computer in 2012) are added to the bride's list of demands. It would typically take an average family around ten years of hard work to save such a large sum. Consequently, to finance a son's wedding, the majority of families, even well-to-do ones, had to incur severe debts. During my fieldwork, I did not hear of any family that did not borrow money to finance a son's wedding.

### Only Leftover Men, No Leftover Women: Women's Upper Hand in the Marriage Market

While the cost of wedding financing has been increasing, young women have gained the upper hand in the sex-ratio imbalanced marriage market. When women take advantage of their leverage and demand high amounts of bridewealth, it further exacerbates the already heavy burden of wedding financing. China's imbalanced sex ratio among people of marriageable age—the long-term consequence of the traditional preference for sons—has created a marriage squeeze for men. In the competition for brides, rural men have had much more difficulty than urban men because of the practice of "spatial hypergamy" among women (Lavely 1991), in which the majority of rural women prefer to marry a man from wealthier rural or even urban areas as a means of achieving a higher standard of living (Fan and Huang 1998; Han 2009; Lavely 1991; Tan and Short 2004).

The shortage of available women for rural men in the marriage market was evident in Lijia Village. In 2006, the most desirable ages for marriage were between nineteen and twenty-one for a woman and between twenty and twenty-two for a man.[5] A man older than twenty-five was considered to be too old for a desirable match (*guogangle*) and faced difficulty in finding a desirable marriage partner. In 2006, almost all Lijia women between the ages of twenty-six and fifty were married. A few divorced or widowed women were either waiting for a suitable match or chose to remain unmarried. Even a few women who were considered not desirable for marriage because they were physically handicapped or mentally challenged were married. In contrast, there were twenty-five bachelors between the ages of twenty-six and fifty, including sixteen who had never been married. "Only leftover men, no leftover women" (*youshengnan, meishengnu*) is how Lijia villagers describe this imbalance. The Chinese state, media, and popular culture also give single urban professional women in their late twenties or older the derogatory *shengnu* (leftover women) label (Fincher 2014; To 2015; Zhang and Sun 2014). While the social stigmatization of single urban women and rural men reveals the enduring significance of marriage in China, the gendered connotations differ for the two groups. Discrimination against urban, professional, and well-educated women past their late twenties reveals the overwhelming emphasis on youth and fulfillment of domestic responsibilities as the ideal standard for a wife, whereas the social exclusion of rural bachelors demonstrates the significance of wealth in determining an ideal husband.

While the marriage squeeze has forced young men into competition for brides, young rural women have gained the upper hand in negotiating marriages. In Lijia Village, once a young woman and a young man agree to continue a relationship after the initial introduction and the visit of the young woman and her family to the young man's house, the man's family asks the woman for her demands for a wedding. The young woman then gives the man's family a list, including the amount for bridewealth, jewelry, a motorcycle, several household items, and sometimes ownership of a house. In recent years only a few young women have asked for a smaller than average amount of bridewealth or agreed to reduce the requested amount. In these cases, the couple have usually met each other at the workplace and developed a mutual affection that led to a marriage proposal. Even in these cases, the groom's family often arranges for a respected relative or family friend to serve as a go-between to facilitate the negotiations. If the man's parents agree to the requests, the couple soon becomes engaged. In most cases, however, a man's family is reluctant to agree to the amount of bridewealth requested and will negotiate for a reduction. If a woman refuses to reduce her request, a man's family has the choice of either accepting the request or withdrawing the marriage proposal. The majority of parents accept the request because they know that they are very likely to face the same situation with another marriage proposal.

In 2006 I closely observed the bridewealth negotiations between Xu Wei's parents and his girlfriend. His parents reluctantly accepted the amount requested after failed negotiations with the young women. Xu Wei was introduced to the young woman by a close relative of his aunt. The matchmaker and the young woman lived in the same village in the township. The couple liked each other after several meetings and were willing to proceed. Xu Wei's parents asked the matchmaker to initiate the marriage proposal on their behalf, and the matchmaker made a phone call to the young woman's house. The following is the conversation between the matchmaker (M) and the young woman (YW).

M: So how much do you ask for?

YW: The same that X [a girl from her village] asked for a while ago.

M: How much is it?

YW: Forty thousand yuan for bridewealth, three pieces of jewelry, and ownership of the house.

M: Any problem with the house?

YW: The house is fine. But if there is any problem [between the young couple and the elderly couple] in the future, they can't kick us out.

M: I'm sure they won't.

YW: And a motorcycle.

M: They have one. Is it OK?

YW: It's all right.

M: Can you ask for a little bit less?

YW: No. If it's acceptable, I'll continue [the relationship]. Otherwise, we are done.

W: Did you discuss it with Xu Wei?

YW: I'm the one who asks for these things. Why should I discuss it with him?

Xu Wei's parents had recently spent all their savings renovating their house and found it extremely difficult to pay the bridewealth. Following the suggestion of a visiting neighbor, Xu Wei called his girlfriend and asked for a reduced amount. To everybody's disappointment, she firmly refused. Frustrated with the large amount, Xu Wei's father suggested that they not proceed with the relationship and that his son find another woman who would ask for less. Disappointed and even outraged, Xu Wei had a harsh verbal confrontation with his father for not being willing to offer the bridewealth to the young woman, whom he really liked. Xu Wei's relatives also supported him and warned his parents that the next woman might ask for even more. Under extreme pressure, Xu Wei's parents finally agreed to borrow money to finance the wedding.

While young women have gained leverage during marriage negotiations, the cost of bridewealth and other wedding expenses as markers of the bride's social value has become the driving force behind the skyrocketing wedding expenses. Like middle-class urban residents whose notion of self-worth has become more based on material possessions than in the past (Li Zhang 2010), the amount of bridewealth offered is equated with the potential bride's worth and how much the groom's family values her. Therefore, young women often compare the amount that other women have requested for the most recent marriage transactions. When others have required a higher amount than they plan to request, prospective brides will try to match it.

In February 2007, a young Lijia woman named Wang Mei was trying to decide whether she should ask for thirty thousand or forty thousand yuan in bridewealth from her boyfriend's family. At that time, thirty thousand yuan was the amount that a few recently married Lijia daughters had requested. When I visited Wang Mei, she asked me about the amount that Xu Wei's girlfriend had requested. I told her that the amount was forty thousand yuan.[6] She promptly replied: "She asked for forty thousand yuan. I will ask for the same amount." The next day, Wang Mei and a few family members went to meet the matchmaker, Uncle Liu, to discuss the amount. Wang Mei told Uncle Liu that she wanted forty thousand yuan and three pieces of jewelry. On behalf of her boyfriend's family, Uncle Liu suggested that she request the same amount but without any jewelry. Wang Mei refused to compromise. The negotiation was at a stalemate for two hours. Her uncle, the husband of an aunt with whom she was very close, reminded her that she should be flexible to avoid putting Uncle Liu into a difficult situation. Her aunt then suggested that her boyfriend's family offer her forty thousand yuan with one piece of jewelry. Eventually, everyone seemed to be satisfied with this arrangement.

The next day, however, when I visited Wang Mei, she had obviously changed her mind. She blamed her uncle for making the compromise and the matchmaker for negotiating on behalf of her boyfriend's family. "I am going to talk to his parents," she said. "I will just say Uncle Liu was drunk yesterday and told them the wrong amount." When I mentioned that her boyfriend's parents had given her two pieces of clothing during her first visit, she said: "The girls in my restaurant all got money, two hundred, three hundred, or even five hundred yuan when they first visited their boyfriends' families.[7] His parents think that they are being very generous. But every family offers money now." Although her boyfriend's family eventually accepted her initial request, she ended up breaking up with him anyway and soon began dating a coworker.

## The Long-Term Mission of Preparing for a Son's Wedding

Although young people in China have gained autonomy in spouse selection and arranged marriage has faded away (Oxfeld 2010; Yan 2003), helping an unmarried child find an ideal marriage partner at a suitable age and financing the wedding are still considered the responsibility of parents in both urban and rural China (Yan 2003; Zhang and Sun 2014). The majority of Lijia parents with a son take their duty very seriously, regarding it as an indication of their genuine love for their sons and their status as responsible parents. For example, when I extended my congratulations to a Lijia woman on her son's recent graduation from college, his secure job in the city, and her having fulfilled her responsibility in supporting her son through college, she firmly responded: "My duty is not done [haimei wancheng renwu]. I need to arrange for the money to buy my son an apartment in the city for his marriage." Villagers frown on the failure to fulfill this critical parental obligation. In a few cases, the parents did not have the resources to finance a son's wedding, nor were they willing to borrow money and pay off the debt through years of hard work. Other villagers criticized these parents for being irresponsible, lazy, and selfish.

Not only do villagers disapprove of parents who fail to make sacrifices to pay for their son's wedding, bachelors who have passed the most suitable age for marriage sometimes express resentment and even anger toward their parents. In one family, a twenty-five-year-old son was frustrated with his parents for not being able to provide the engagement money to a young woman to whom he was introduced. One day, after a verbal confrontation with his parents, he broke a window in their house and left home. Financing a wedding for a son, then, not only fulfills a crucial parental obligation but also avoids criticism from other villagers and blame from sons.

The heavy financial obligations have created intense pressure and anxiety for couples who have an unmarried son who is getting past the most suitable age for marriage. While parents in urban Shanghai gathered at a park to look for a marriage partner for their unmarried child, turning a personal affair into a public event (Zhang and Sun 2014), Lijia parents whose son is reaching his mid-twenties openly express their concern for his single status. They enthusiastically welcome matchmakers and even eagerly reach out to their relatives and social network to ask for an introduction to suitable prospects for their son. As village endogamy has always been practiced in the village, parents often seriously consider available young Lijia women. When they find a young woman whom they consider suitable, they will ask a close relative or friend who is willing to approach the woman and her parents.

In addition to active involvement in matchmaking, parents who have an unmarried son have to make long-term preparations to finance his wedding. They usually start preparing well in advance, as early as when their son reaches his mid-teens, to balance the large financial burden. Because housing is one of the major and most expensive requirements, preparations start with rebuilding or renovating a house. Parents will renovate a house that is considered in good condition, replacing the doors and windows, redoing the floors, and covering the kitchen and the exterior walls of the house with ceramic tile. For a house that is considered too small or requires major renovations, parents often choose to rebuild it. In those cases, they usually leave parts of the house unfinished such as postponing covering the ceiling or separating a large room into two smaller ones. When a son is ready to marry, the couple will finish the renovation according to the latest fashion. In 2006, four Lijia families either rebuilt or renovated a house. Two of these families had a teenage son; another had a son in his early twenties, and the parents were asking their relatives and friends to introduce him to a young woman. Typically, Lijia parents pay for rebuilding or renovation with their savings and some loans. Once the house is finished, they will spend several years paying off their debts. By then, their son will have reached the age to start to look for a marriage partner. When their son is ready for marriage, they will use their earnings and borrow money from their relatives and friends to pay for bridewealth and other wedding expenses. To pay off all their debts, the parents will have to keep working even after their son's wedding.

The story of Zhao Lan exemplifies the long-term preparations for and the intense pressure from financing a son's wedding. In 2007 Zhao Lan and her husband had a newly married daughter and a teenage son. In preparation for their son's future wedding, they had recently spent a large amount of money rebuilding their house. While I was visiting the family on a spring day in 2007, Zhao Lan gave me a tour of her house and explained in detail the design of each room, the building materials, and even their prices. Deeply impressed with the larger-than-average size of the house—the floor plan of which followed the most recent local style, the elegantly tiled indoor floors and internal and external walls, and the kitchen, which was carefully designed for functionality—I told Zhao Lan that she and her husband must be proud of building such a stylish home. While showing pride, she also complained about the efforts that she and her husband had made and her anxiety about financing her son's future wedding. "Since my son was born," she said, "I have felt a big mountain over my head. After building the house, I feel I can take a breath temporarily. We will have to continue to work hard to make money for his wedding. . . . When I gave birth to my son, ten thousand yuan was absolutely enough for a son's wedding. Now it is so much more, and who knows how much more it will be when my son is ready to marry. . . . If we don't pay for his wedding, people will look down on us, and even our children will look down on us." She went on to say that she had told her son that "in the past, the Japanese [soldiers] forced people [Chinese civilians] to work for them, pointing guns at their [the civilians'] backs. You are exactly like the Japanese [forcing me to work for you]!" [8]

To prepare financially for a son's wedding, couples with an unmarried son need to plan their budgets carefully. Lijia couples who take their parental responsibilities seriously have to refrain from spending beyond their daily needs. The conscientious planning of the family budget is demonstrated by a conversation among a group of Lijia women that I observed in spring 2007. During that time, a type of golden ring, locally referred to as lucky ring (*zhuanyunzhu*), had become a new fashion among women in the area. A local practice later evolved in which a mother-in-law bought such a ring as a gift to a young daughter-in-law. Some middle-aged women started to follow the trend and bought a ring for themselves. While the group encouraged a woman who had a twenty-two-year-old unmarried son to buy a ring, she responded: "I'm not buying one. I have a big debt (*dajihuang*) at home [referring to her son's future wedding finance]." Another woman, whose unmarried son was the same age and who had recently completed renovating her house in preparation for her son's future wedding, immediately followed: "If my child were a girl, I would definitely have had bought one already." For these two women, making financial preparations for their son's future wedding took priority over making fashionable purchases.

## Serving Sons and Daughters-in-Law after Their Wedding

Parental obligations do not end with a son's wedding ceremony. After the wedding, the groom's parents are expected to continue to offer help with household chores, childcare, and financial support. As noted in chapter 4, under the renegotiated logic of intergenerational exchange, an elderly couple must make an effort to establish a harmonious relationship with their son and daughter-in-law in the hope that the young couple will appreciate their efforts and reciprocate by taking care of them when they are old. Another factor contributing to the expectation for parental support on the part of a man's family is young women's upper hand in marital conflicts and termination—a continuation of young women's increased leverage in the marriage market. Consequently, not only are parents obligated to pay for a son's wedding, they also have to help maintain their son's marriage, which they already have financed through years of hard work.

China's long-standing patrilineal and patriarchal tradition generally prohibited women from initiating a divorce, and once widowed or divorced by a husband, women were discouraged from remarrying (Stacey 1983, 34).[9] The social prohibition against a woman's initiating a divorce and remarrying continued after 1949. According to my interviews with elderly Lijia residents, in the 1950s, despite the passage of the Marriage Law, which granted women the right to initiate a divorce, they had heard of only a few women in the township area who took advantage of their newly granted right and initiated a divorce. It was not until the 1990s that divorce was tolerated, especially among young villagers. Nowadays, villagers offered moral support to women who suffered domestic violence from their husbands or parents-in-laws and, refusing to tolerate living in an unhappy marriage, sought a divorce. In the summer of 2005, a Lijia woman left her husband without notice after he had

**Table 7** Divorces from a first marriage in Lijia Village, late 1980s–2006

| Year | Cause of marriage termination |
|------|-------------------------------|
| Late 1980s | Wife had an affair and initiated a divorce |
| 1991 | Divorced shortly after marriage; unclear who initiated the divorce |
| 1994 | Wife beating; wife initiated a divorce |
| 1996 | Wife had an affair and divorced to marry the man |
| 1997 | Wife left for a Lijia bachelor |
| | Wife had an affair; unclear who initiated the divorce |
| 1998 | Wife left for a Lijia bachelor |
| 1999 | Wife had an affair and divorced to marry the man |
| 2000 | Wife had an affair and initiated a divorce |
| 2005 | Marital conflicts; unclear who initiated the divorce |
| | Wife beating; wife left without notice |
| | Family conflicts; wife initiated the divorce |
| | Wife had an affair and initiated the divorce |
| 2006 | Wife beating; wife left without notice |

severely beaten her. The majority of the villagers I interviewed supported her choice because she was not treated with respect by her husband and her father-in-law, even though she was considered a hard worker. A young married man told me angrily: "This kind of man should remain a bachelor for the rest of his life!" The change in public opinion has removed the barrier to women's initiating a divorce. Because of the imbalanced sex ratio among people of marriageable age, a woman can easily remarry if she chooses. For a second marriage, a woman can still demand bridewealth, although it is usually less than the amount for a first marriage. In addition, because women can always find nonagricultural employment, they no longer have to be confined to their community or depend on their husbands for a living.

Like the majority of divorces in urban areas (Woo 2006), in Lijia Village, except for three cases in which the initiator was unclear, the fourteen divorces from a first marriage in Lijia Village between the late 1980s and 2006 were initiated by wives (see Table 7).[10] Domestic violence was involved in most of the divorces, including three cases in which wife beating was the direct cause. Women refused to put up with an unhappy marriage and chose to leave their husbands, especially after they had found new love, as was the case in seven of the fourteen cases.

In comparison to a woman's divorce, a divorce tends to be devastating for a man because he not only faces an enormous financial loss but also risks returning to the disgraced social category of a bachelor for the rest of his life. The difficulty of remarriage for a divorced man is illustrated by the fourteen divorce cases listed in table 7. Of the fourteen men, only six had remarried by 2007. Among these six cases, two of the new marriages ended a few years later—one ended when the wife left for another man; the other ended when the wife committed suicide. In addition to these fourteen divorces, in a few families, a man took back his wife, who had left him for another man and later returned to him.

To keep his marriage intact, not only does a man have to learn to treat his wife with respect, but his parents have to make a contribution by offering physical and financial assistance to the young couple during the early years of their marriage. After a son's wedding, the young couple typically lives with the husband's parents, and they have meals together for as long as the young couple and the elderly couple find this living arrangement feasible. The elderly parents often take a larger share than the young couple of such household chores as preparing meals and cleaning rooms. A few years after the wedding, a young couple will usually decide to live independently. Among young couples who share a yard with the husband's parents, the elderly couple often takes over shared household chores, such as cleaning the yard and outdoor toilet and tending the vegetable garden. After a grandchild is born, the husband's parents are expected to provide childcare during the child's early years. If the daughter-in-law works during the day, the grandparents become the major caregivers for the grandchild.

In addition to providing assistance with household chores and childcare, some elderly parents also offer financial support when a young couple is going through a financial crisis. In 2006 and 2007, a type of underground lottery became popular in the area, and a large number of villagers participated. As a result, many villagers were trapped in varying amounts of debt. This financial crisis caused marital conflicts among a few young couples. The wives from two families in which the husband incurred severe gambling debts were so frustrated and furious that they demanded a divorce. In one of these families, the man's parents, who were well off, paid their son's debts to save his marriage.

## The Fear of Sons

Because of the exorbitant cost of wedding financing and the continuing efforts to help a son's family after his wedding, a son has become a financial burden for his parents. Some middle-aged and elderly couples who made the decision to have a second child expressed bitterness and even regret about their decision. The story of Liu Hua, a Lijia woman in her fifties shows how the recent dramatic increase in the cost of wedding financing and the continuing obligation to help a son after his wedding have transformed a son from a source of joy into a cause of frustration. Liu Hua and her husband had their first child, a daughter, in the mid-1970s. Liu Hua became pregnant in 1980, right after the one-child rule began to be enforced. She and her husband soon became the target of the birth-planning officials, who demanded she have an abortion. The couple was required to attend education meetings every day and was threatened with a severe fine if they did not comply. The officials even ordered the township clinic not to deliver her baby if they continued with the pregnancy. Determined to have a second child, they eventually had to ask Liu Hua's mother to take the risk of delivering the baby. When they found out that the baby was a boy, they were so happy that they believed all their efforts had been worth it. To express her joy and satisfaction with the birth of a boy, Liu Hua's mother-in-law named the boy Kexin, meaning "as they wished."

The story had taken quite a turn, however, when I met Liu Hua in 2006. Her son had been recently divorced, and she had become the primary caregiver for her two-year-old granddaughter while her husband and her son worked to support the family. As she was complaining to me about the everyday burden of taking care of her granddaughter with her eyesight failing and debts remaining from her son's wedding a few years earlier, she said with deep frustration: "Sometimes I am so mad at my husband. He was the one who wanted a second child. What is the use of having a son? It is not *kexin*, but *naoxin* [upsetting]!"

While some middle-aged and elderly couples express strong resentment over their choice to have a second child who has turned out to require a large amount of financial support, young couples who have a singleton daughter have developed a fear of sons, which discourages them from making the decision to have a second child. As young Lijia couples have engendered the transformation of old-age support provided by sons and this gendered shift of filial piety has had a significant impact on their decision not to have a second child, these couples, young women in particular, are also the driving force behind the increasing burden of wedding financing. They are thus well aware of the power dynamic in the negotiation of marriage proposals and understand that the financial burden is ever increasing and unavoidable. According to these young couples, because they cannot predict the sex of an unborn child, they fear that a second birth might result in a boy, which would impose a heavy burden on them for many years to come. Because these young parents have experienced the increasing financial demands for childrearing and maintaining a modern lifestyle, those who do not have a strong preference for a son eventually make the decision to be content with a singleton daughter.

## Conclusion

A man's marriage is significant because it not only offers him companionship but also establishes his status in his community. At the same time, the patrilineal practice of expecting the groom's family to shoulder the responsibility of wedding financing has persisted. In the sex-ratio imbalanced marriage market, young women have gained the upper hand in negotiating marriage proposals and are able to exercise their agency by demanding a large amount of bridewealth, thus exacerbating the financial burden on the groom's family. Not only are parents expected by their sons and their community to fulfill this critical parental obligation, they must continue supporting their sons and daughters-in-law after the wedding to help maintain their sons' marriage, all of which requires years of hard work. Consequently, a son has become a financial burden for his parents.

The changing role of sons from a source of support in old age to a financial burden has contributed to a decline in the deeply ingrained tradition of preference for sons among Chinese families. While the expenses of childrearing have significantly increased as a result of the rising cost of a child's consumption and education, raising a son now requires additional long-term financial obligations. As young couples have focused their financial resources and time on the pursuit of a new life ideal and childrearing practice, they are reluctant to take on the heavy and unavoidable parental responsibility for a son. Thus, some young couples have decided to limit themselves to a singleton daughter.

# 6

## Emerging from the Ancestors' Shadow
### *The Weakened Belief in Family Continuity*

ON A LUNAR NEW YEAR'S DAY in the mid-1980s, an elderly Lijia man who had four sons and three grandsons posted a couplet that he had carefully composed (a tradition in China for the holiday celebration) prominently on the gate of his yard. The couplet proudly demonstrates his ideal for family prosperity: "horses and vehicles in front of a house do not signal wealth; sons and grandsons at home do not count as poverty [*menqian chema feiweigui; jiayou zisun busuanpin*]." His couplet deeply hurt the feelings of his oldest daughter-in-law, who had given birth to two daughters. When she took her daughters to visit her parents-in-law for New Year's greetings and saw what her father-in-law had written, she felt as if she were being insulted because she had failed to produce a son.

She gave birth to her first daughter in 1980, the first year the one-child policy was enforced in Lijia Village. Four years later, she and her husband became one of two Lijia couples who were allowed to have a second child when the one-child rule was first relaxed. The official rationale was that the woman's widowed mother did not have a son, and the couple was committed to taking on the responsibility of supporting the elderly mother. The wife became pregnant after obtaining a second-child permit and had an ultrasound. To everyone's disappointment, she was carrying a girl. She did not want to endure the physical suffering of an abortion and another birth that trying to have a son would bring, so she strongly resisted her husband's demand for an abortion and even threatened divorce. In 1985, she gave birth to her second daughter. When I interviewed her in 2007, her older daughter, now twenty-seven, had completed her education in a vocational school and landed a secure, well-paid job as a schoolteacher in the county seat. Her younger daughter was a college student, a highly admired achievement in the village. The mother told me with pride: "All of my husband's brothers and sisters have a son. We're the only family that doesn't have one. In the past, my mother-in-law used to curse me, saying *juehou* [family line finished] when we had a conflict. Now look at her grandsons. None of them is successful. Seeing that we're doing so well, my mother-in-law has to admit that daughters can be good." The youngest son of the elderly man who wrote the couplet shared the Lijia woman's view. He was a forty-year-old married man who had a singleton son in 2007. When he told me about his father's couplet and the childbearing preference among villagers of his parents' generation, he commented: "Nowadays, nobody shares my father's belief any more. If you're not rich, even if you have sons and grandsons, you're still considered poor."

The story of this Lijia family reveals two very different views of son preference and family prosperity. The elderly father who wrote the couplet and the elderly mother who cursed her sonless daughter-in-law believed that producing sons to continue the ancestral line was a critical indicator of family prosperity and pride, following the long-standing tradition among Chinese families. Indeed, the continuity of the patrilineage was so significant for a Chinese person's identity and socioeconomic well-being that anthropologist Francis Hsu (1948) described the Chinese as living "under the ancestors' shadow." The oldest daughter-in-law and the youngest son in this family, by contrast, no longer associated having a son to pass on the family line with family pride and prosperity. The oldest daughter-in-law considered her daughters' success in securing a well-paid job and a college education a source of pride, and the youngest son regarded financial affluence as the only criteria for family prosperity.

This chapter delves into the transformation of another critical factor contributing to China's deeply rooted tradition of son preference: the cultural, religious, and social significance of having a son to pass on the patrilineal ancestral line. It first discusses the ways in which the preference for sons and related practices have declined among young Lijia couples and then explores three interrelated factors that have contributed to the changes. First, on the institutional and cultural level, while the belief in the continuity of the family line is often strong with a well-developed lineage organization, in Lijia Village the history of migration, state attacks on lineage development, and the lack of a lineage culture have played a role in the weakened belief in having a son to pass on the family line. Second, on the religious level, although the concepts of an afterlife and a reciprocal relation between ancestors and their living descendants have deeply shaped the traditional belief system of the Chinese, such beliefs are now subject to skepticism among young Lijia villagers. Third, and most important, on the social and communal level, while having a son to continue the family line used to define a family's and individual's status in the community, the basis of social status has shifted from producing sons to earning money, significantly undermining the preference for a son among young Lijia couples. The changing values have removed the stigma attached to families without a son and encouraged young couples to embrace a singleton daughter.

## Passing on the Household Registration Booklet

The priority given to the continuity of the patrilineal ancestral line once shaped the kinship organization, belief system, and socialization of children among Chinese families (Hsu 1948). In the patrilineal tradition, sons are significant because only a son could pass on the family line. Having at least one male heir was such a vital life goal that families who were unable to produce a son tried alternatives, such as adoption—a form of "manipulated kinship" (Zhenman Zheng 2001). When an adoption was arranged, the adopted son would take his adoptive father's surname. His duties of filial piety and ancestor worship were thus transferred from his birth parents to his adoptive parents (Jordan 1972, 90–91; Waltner 1990; Wolf and Huang 1980). In many cases, a couple would adopt a son from their closest agnates in the descending generation, a practice called *guoji* (J. Watson 1975). An old saying among Lijia villagers vividly expresses the significance of the role of a son in family continuity: "A family needs to have someone pooping on the bed and someone visiting the grave and burning spirit money for the ancestors" (*kangshang deyou lashide, fenshang deyou shaozhide*). "Someone" undoubtedly refers to a son. According to elderly Lijia villagers, in the past, a son was thus referred to as *shangfen shaozhide*, which literally means "one who visits the grave and burns spirit money" for the ancestors.

The birth of a son was thus a cause for celebration. A woman told me that when the health practitioner at the township birth-planning clinic delivered her son in the 1980s, she immediately told her the good news: "It's a *daxi* [big happiness]." A reception usually followed a month after the birth of a baby boy, when relatives and friends congratulated the family with monetary gifts. The birth of a girl, in contrast, brought disappointment. A woman who gave birth to a girl at home in 1996 told me: "After the baby was delivered, the two women in the room were quiet. I knew immediately that it was a girl. My father-in-law was disappointed and didn't come to see my daughter until several days later. He was so disappointed that his throat was swollen and he wasn't able to talk for a couple of days!"

During my fieldwork, the expression describing a son's role had changed from "visiting the grave and burning spirit money" to "passing on the household registration booklet [*jiehukoubende*]." The household registration booklet, issued by the local police station, records demographic information and family relations for each household member. The registration system is a form of administrative control that has been enforced since the 1950s. A daughter typically transfers her registration to her husband's household upon marriage, whereas a son keeps his registration and adds his wife to the booklet when he marries and his child's when the child is born, hence the phrase, "someone to pass on the household registration booklet." It is interesting to note that the new phrase reveals the imprint of state governance on villagers' understanding of a son's role in family continuity, whereas the older phrase emphasizes his cultural and religious significance in family continuity.

Along with the shift in local phrase for a son, the significance of family continuity has noticeably declined. Although young villagers

still celebrate the birth of a son, they no longer share the older generation's belief that having a son and maintaining family continuity is indispensable. Families without a son very rarely express concern and anxiety about family continuity. When I asked villagers who did not have a
son about family continuity, a typical response was "It's no use worrying
about whether I should have a son to pass on the household registration
booklet to. Now every family has only one child. Even though I have a
son there's no guarantee that my son will have a son." Meanwhile, the
birth of a girl is welcomed with joy and celebration. Some families also
host a reception a month after the birth of a girl. The remainder of this
chapter focuses on the ways in which a lack of a lineage culture, increasing skepticism concerning ancestor worship, and the changing markers
of social status have contributed to the decline in the importance of having a son to continue the family line among young Lijia villagers.

## Lineage Culture and Family Continuity

Lineage organization, which flourished under the influence of neo-
Confucian scholar-bureaucrats, was the basic social structure of traditional Han Chinese society (Szonyi 2002; Zhenman Zheng 2001). Well-
developed lineage organizations played a significant role in the life of an
individual and in society at large (Baker 1968, 1979; Cohen 2005; Eastman 1988; Freedman 1966; Szonyi 2002; R. S. Watson 1986; Zhenman
Zheng 2001). In South China highly institutionalized lineages served
as the basic economic unit for production and consumption and as the
fundamental organization for political authority and educational, ritual,
and cultural activities (Zhenman Zheng 2001). Under the strong lineage
culture, producing male heirs not only contributed to the continuity of
a lineage but also granted a family lasting membership in a lineage and
full participation in lineage activities.

Lineage organizations came under attack during the collective period and were replaced by grassroots administration (Baker 1979; Potter
and Potter 1990). In South China, where the attacks were severe, lineage
properties were confiscated, ancestral halls destroyed or occupied by
the government, genealogy books burned, and ancestral tablets hidden
(Oxfeld 2010; Parish and Whyte 1978; Peng 2011). Radical state policy

against lineage organizations did not, however, eliminate lineage culture. Since the 1980s, when the government relaxed its control over cultural and religious practices, lineage organizations in Southeast China have been revived, ancestral tombs and ancestral halls rebuilt, genealogies recompiled, and grave visits resumed (Friedman 2006; Ma 2002; Peng 2011; Potter and Potter 1990).

In North China, since the tenth century, as a result of political instability, low population density, and economic conditions, lineage organizations survived in "a more diluted and weakened form" (Peng 2011). They tended to be smaller, possessed fewer corporate estates, and were not as effectively organized as those in South China (Rawski 1986). In Northeast China, lineage culture was even weaker because the majority of residents are descendants of migrants from North China who settled the region during the middle and late nineteenth century (Gottschang and Lary 2000). The early settlers severed ties with their lineages in their home communities and were unable to develop enough genealogical depth to form lineage organizations in their new homeland. After 1949, with the state attacks on lineage organizations and ancestral rituals, budding agnatic groups did not have the resources and institutional support to fully develop into lineage organizations.

Among the earliest settlers in Lijia Village was the Wang family, a couple who migrated from Shandong Province with their children in the mid-nineteenth century. By the late 1940s and the early 1950s, the Wangs had grown into one of two largest agnatic groups in the village. Members of the group organized informal group activities. Fourth-generation wives would offer a collective Lunar New Year's greetings to the elderly members in the group, and on the marriage of a male member the wives would be sent to greet the new bride. The Wang's agnatic group, however, never owned collective property for joint economic activities or an ancestral hall that symbolized their lineage organization. Recording the family genealogy on ancestral scrolls was the only practice representing the continuity of the agnatic group.

During my fieldwork in Lijia Village, the lineage concept was of little significance to villagers. In other regions in rural North and Northeast China, after the relaxation of state control over ancestral rituals, performing the rituals became a matter for individual families rather than an activity organized by lineages (Kipnis 1997; Yan 1996). Similarly, in Lijia Village, there had not been organized ancestral rituals and group activities within an agnatic group since the relaxation of state control. Instead, villagers would practice grave visits and celebrate important holidays within their nuclear or extended families. For example, I celebrated Lunar New Year's Eve in 2007 with two Lijia families. In one family, the husband was one of six sons. His wife and daughter had dinner with his widowed mother, the family of his oldest brother, and a bachelor brother. The other three brothers celebrated the day with their wives and children. In the second family, the elderly couple had two sons. They spent the day with their widowed younger son and a granddaughter, with whom they shared a yard. Their older son and his wife stayed at home and had dinner with their son's family.[1]

In the village, along with the shift in the practice of ancestral rituals and celebration of holidays, the practice of keeping and displaying an ancestral scroll has declined measurably. During the Cultural Revolution, keeping an ancestral scroll was forbidden and villagers were asked to burn their scrolls. A few families took a risk, hiding their scroll during the government campaigns, and were thus able to save it, whereas most others no longer had their original scroll. In 2007, only twenty-one households still adhered in varying degrees to the tradition of keeping and displaying an ancestral scroll. A few families had paid someone to draw a scroll and wrote down the names of their ancestors based on their memories (see fig. 8). Five of these families simply used a piece of red paper with words such as "the five generations of the Wang family" to represent an ancestral scroll (see fig. 9). Some families only display their scroll on Lunar New Year's Day. Among these twenty-one families, all except one were elderly villagers. The one couple in their forties prominently displayed the husband's ancestral scroll, which he had paid someone to paint, but it only recorded three generations. Interestingly, they were one of two Lijia couples who had a third and unauthorized child in an attempt to have a son. While showing me his ancestral scroll, the husband said to me: "I am old-minded. I want to have a son to pass on my family line."

An active lineage culture, in which members contribute either labor or money to building an ancestral hall or compile a genealogy, is as-

**Figure 8.** An ancestral altar with an ancestral scroll hung by an elderly couple on the wall, 2006. The elderly man paid someone to paint the scroll and wrote down the names of his ancestors based on his memory. The altar on the left was dedicated to the God of Fortune.

sociated with son preference (Murphy, Tao, and Lu 2011). Without a well-developed lineage organization, there are no incentives to produce male heirs to fully participate in group activities to gain economic cooperation and social support. Because young couples form their own social network through affinal relatives and friends, they no longer solely rely on a patrilineal kinship group for such activities. In addition, without a strong lineage organization or a solidified agnatic group, there is no institutionalized lineage authority that regulates the behavior of its members by, for example, pressuring members to produce male heirs. Furthermore, in Southeast China, where lineage organizations have been revived following the relaxation of state-imposed rules, not only do many lineage members continue to hold a preference for a son but lineages serve as strong support networks for members to circumvent or resist the implementation of the birth-planning policy (Peng 2011). For example, in rural Jiangxi, when village officials tracked down a woman

**Figure 9.** An ancestral altar set up by an elderly couple for the Lunar New Year, 2007. There is red paper in the frame, which represents an ancestral scroll of the elderly wife's natal family, with the phrase "the five generations of the Zhu family." The wife shared an intimate tie with her natal parents and her husband supported her setting up an ancestor altar for them, a practice that would have been forbidden in the past. To the right of the altar is a framed picture of Guanyin.

who had an unauthorized pregnancy and was hiding in her natal village, male members from the woman's natal lineage supported her and physically attacked the officials (ibid.). Without strong support from a lineage, couples would often have to yield to the authority of a powerful state. Demographic data further reveals the link between the strength of a lineage culture and the degree of son preference. In Southeast and Central China, where lineage culture is strong, high birthrates and male-biased sex ratios at birth have been reported, whereas in the Northeast, Southwest, and the Yangtze River area, where villages have a relatively short history and lineage culture is weak, birthrates have been low and sex ratios at birth more balanced than in other regions (Gong, Duan, and Wu 2013; Peng 2011).

## Skepticism about the Practice of Ancestor Worship

The practice of ancestor worship is the "concrete expression of this [the Chinese] preoccupation with the patriline" (J. Watson 1988, 8), which shaped the cultural and religious significance of the son's role within Chinese families. Ancestor worship, or "the cult of the dead" (Ahern 1973), is a hybridized belief and practice that combines the Confucian ideal of filial piety with Buddhist teachings about salvation and reincarnation, indigenous ideas associated with shamanism and geomancers, and beliefs about the underworld (Ahern 1973; Ebrey 1991; Oxfeld 2004). The belief is based on the concept of an afterlife in which spirit of a deceased enters into the underworld, in which spirits have emotions, such as pleasure and anger, and are subject to the same needs as humans, such as food, clothing, and money (Baker 1979). Rather than being severed by death, deceased ancestors and their descendants engage in a reciprocal relationship through ancestral rituals: ancestors need the worship and offerings from their descendants, and descendants need the blessing and support from their ancestors, who have the supernatural power to intervene in the lives of the living (Ahern 1973; Baker 1979).

Ancestors' names were traditionally inscribed on tablets and placed on domestic altars or recorded on a scroll, in front of which their descents performed ancestral rituals on certain occasions (Eastman 1988; Jordan 1972). Another major ancestral ritual is the grave visit, during which descendants send offerings to their ancestors through burning spirit money and various paper goods, such as replicas of clothes and houses (Ahern 1973). In Lijia Village, there are four occasions for grave visits: Lunar New Year's Day; the Qingming Festival, the day for cleaning ancestors' graves; July 15 by the lunar calendar, the day when the gate to the underworld is believed to be held open for ancestors to receive offerings; and October 1 by the lunar calendar, the day for sending warm winter clothes to ancestors.

Ancestral rituals were traditionally performed by male descendants and their wives (Baker 1968; Freedman 1966). Because a married daughter joined her husband's patrilineage, she had no obligation to practice ancestor worship for her father's lineage. When ancestral rituals were performed, strict rules were applied to family members and outsiders. In Lijia Village, a married daughter was not allowed to visit her natal family until the sixth day of Lunar New Year, when the ancestral altar had been put away. Violating the rule was believed to inflict misfortune on the family because a married daughter was considered an outsider and would bring bad luck to her natal family if she saw the ancestral altar.

The only way to achieve ancestor status and secure a good afterlife was to have at least one male heir. Thus, people tried all means to produce a son.[2] Several elderly Lijia villagers told me the story of Old Wang to explain the necessity of having a male heir to practice ancestral rituals and the anxiety a sonless person could experience. One day in the early 1950s, when Lijia villagers were burning spirit money for their deceased ancestors, Old Wang, an elderly bachelor, burned spirit money with his own name written on it.[3] When asked why he was burning spirit money for himself, he answered: "I don't have a son to send me money after I die. So I send some money to the underworld now and save it there for myself. After I die and go to the underworld, I'll have money to spend."

Since the early 1960s, a series of government campaigns targeted ancestor worship, attacking it as superstitious and backward. Villagers recalled that during the "Four Cleanups" (*siqing*) movement in the mid-1960s, a work team sent by the upper government stayed in the village to enforce the banning of ancestral rituals. Burning spirit money was strictly forbidden. Before traditional grave visit days, villagers were called to attend education meetings at which officials reiterated the ban on burning spirit money. After the work team left, the village and township officials continued to enforce the ban.

Officials made a distinction between grave visits as a fitting way to commemorate deceased family members and burning spirit money as a backward and superstitious practice. They told villagers that grave visits with proper practices, such as clearing the weeds and bowing to show respect to deceased family members, were acceptable. The government even organized students to pay homage in a nearby cemetery dedicated to soldiers who died in the county during the 1945–48 civil war. The government education on proper practices during grave visits confused some villagers, who believed that the very purpose of grave visits was to send money to deceased ancestors. In an interview, one villager expressed his confusion: "I asked an official from the work team why visiting ancestors' graves was superstitious while visiting the cemetery was not. I was told that it was all right to visit the ancestors' graves to just clear the weeds and bow to the graves. But burning spirit money was superstitious." Although some villagers secretly burned spirit money during grave visits, using yellow wrapping paper from a shop and imprinting the shape of coins on the paper, some villagers stopped visiting ancestral graves because of the ban. They even joked that "the living are poor. So it is all right that the dead are poor too."

Starting in the 1980s, the ban on ancestral rituals was relaxed. Although grave visits and burning spirit money have been revived, the practices remain "disjointed and highly fragmented in both belief and performance" (Jankowiak 1993, 266), and the impact of ancestor worship on the lives of peasants seems to have diminished (Parish and Whyte 1978). Like other regions of rural and urban China (Jankowiak 1993; Yan 2003), the belief in the afterlife declined among Lijia villagers. In my interviews, some older Lijia villagers expressed doubt, while many young villagers were more outspoken in expressing their lack of belief in an afterlife. One twenty-seven-year-old woman said: "The dumbest person knows that after death a person is just a pile of ash after cremation."[4]

Many villagers also have mixed motivations for their performance of ancestral rituals. Most villagers believe that grave visits and burning spirit money are a way to commemorate deceased family members. Like villagers in rural Guangdong who differentiate remembrance from be-lief in an afterlife and ancestral spirits (Oxfeld 2010), some Lijia villag-ers who express their disbelief in an afterlife emphasize "remembrance" as the motivation behind their practice. A young Lijia man told me why he visited his grandparents' graves: "I don't believe in an afterlife. My grandparents treated me very well when they were alive. I visit their graves to pay my respect and show my filiality to them." In addition to commemorating deceased family members, some villagers still be-lieve that burning spirit money is a way to send money to their ances-tors and ask for blessings, especially when they or their family members have health issues. One Lijia woman told me after her visit to her father-in-law's grave: "I had a sore throat in the last few days and it would not go away. Last night, I had a dream that my father-in-law didn't have any shirt on [meaning her father-in-law needed warm clothes]. Now, after I have burned some money for him, my sore throat is gone."

The most important motivation for grave visits, however, which the majority of villagers share, is to avoid criticism from other villagers; in other words, by "putting on a show for the living" (huoren yanmu). During grave visits, villagers put a piece of spirit money under a rock on top of the grave to show to other villagers that someone in the fam-ily had visited their ancestor's grave (see fig. 10). Because villagers are fa-miliar with the locations of the graves of other families, they could eas-ily identify a family that did not visit their ancestor's grave by checking whether there was a piece of spirit money on top of the grave. Villagers who do not visit their ancestors' graves would be criticized for being un-filial. Some villagers told me frankly that they practiced grave visits to follow the trend (suidaliu) and would stop the practice if no one else in the village did it any more.

A Lijia man in his late fifties was skeptical about the practice of grave visits and the belief in ancestor worship: "To be honest, visiting graves and burning spirit money are just to put a show to the living. My son once asked me after we burned spirit money at my grandparents' grave whether they would receive the spirit money that was put on the grave. I told him that those papers were just to show to the living and would not be received." I asked him whether he believed that his grand-parents would receive the spirit money he had burned. He jokingly re-

**Figure 10.** Grave visit of a father and his oldest son, 2006. The two men are burning spirit money for the elderly man's parents.

plied: "Who knows? I sent so much spirit money to my grandparents, but I've never received a single letter from them. Who knows whether they ever received the money?" He then continued: "I do it so that nobody can criticize me for being unfilial."

Funerals are another occasion for putting on a display to impress other villagers. Some families hire a band for a deceased parent's funeral. The band will play loud popular music during the day and traditional funeral songs in the evening. Villagers gather in the family's yard in the evening to watch the performance. As has been observed elsewhere in rural China (Xin Liu 2000; Oxfeld 2004), putting a grand show at a funeral nowadays is a public display of filiality and wealth and reflected "only the relationship among the living themselves" (Xin Liu 2000, 153). Several villagers told me that some of the families who hire a band for a deceased parent's funeral were not filial at all when the parent was alive. A local saying criticizes this practice as "being unfilial when parents were alive, yet crying loudly after their deaths [*huozhe buxiao sile luanjiao*]."[5] An elderly woman expressed her disapproval: "I say this to my children all the time. I ask them how much money they plan to spend on my funeral. I tell them just to give the money to me, and I'll spend it when I'm still alive. No need to spend money on my funeral. It's all a show for the living. When a person dies, it's just like a lamp burned out [*rensi rudengmie*]."

While villagers expressed mixed motivations behind practicing ancestral rituals, the gendered practice of ancestral rituals has undergone significant shifts. Some rules that forbid a married daughter at the rituals in her natal family are no longer observed. For example, a married daughter was no longer barred from visiting her natal family until the altar was removed after Lunar New Year. In fact, the majority of Lijia families no longer set up an altar for the New Year celebration any more. On Lunar New Year's Day in 2007, I encountered several married daughters living in Lijia Village who were visiting their parents early in the morning. In one family, the daughter was playing poker with her father and her siblings right in front of the ancestral altar.

Along with the relaxed rules on ritual observance, a large number of married daughters have visited their deceased parents' graves. Although in the past villagers believed that the spirit money that a married daughter burned would not be received by her parents because she was now an outsider, many villagers nowadays believe that there is no difference between a son's and a married daughter's practice. Some villagers said: "Daughters are children too. When a daughter burns spirit money for her deceased parents, why won't the money be received?" Some married daughters returned to Lijia Village to visit their deceased parents' graves, while some women who married into Lijia Village went back to their natal village during the traditional occasions for grave visits. Others, whose natal family was too far away, chose not to return and burned spirit money at a crossroad.[6] A visit that the Lu family organized to their deceased father's grave on the day before the Qingming Festival in 2007 provides an example of a daughter's participation. Among the six sons in the family, one son visited the grave by himself early in the morning, two bachelor sons were working outside the village, and three daughters-in-law visited the grave together in place of their husbands who were working in the city. The older daughter, who lived in Lijia Village, and the younger daughter, who lived in a different village, also participated in the grave visit. Even the younger son-in-law, who drove his wife to the village on his motorcycle, participated in the grave visit.

The transformations in the belief and practice of ancestor worship have significantly affected the belief among young Lijia couples that having a son to perform ancestral rituals was indispensable. Those who were skeptical about the idea of an afterlife and a reciprocal relationship between ancestors and living descendants had little motivation to prepare for their own afterlife. Therefore, these young couples did not feel strongly about needing a son to practice ancestor worship after their deaths. Further, once a daughter's role in grave visits was recognized and accepted, a daughter could fill the role previously reserved for a son, taking care of family graves and performing ancestral rituals.

## A New Status Marker

Another critical factor contributing to the traditional need for a son is that family continuity defined the status of a family and an individual in a community. While the state attacks on ancestor worship challenged the religious and cultural significance of the role of sons, the socioeconomic transformations resulting from decollectivization and subsequent market reforms starting in the early 1980s have further shaken family continuity as the most significant marker of social status in village life.

In the patrilineal tradition, families without a male heir were regarded with pity and sometimes even stigmatized by their community. The birth of a girl, therefore, brought disappointment, frustration, and even humiliation to her parents. In late imperial times, a woman who gave birth to a female infant had to endure "the oppression of bystanders" (King 2014, 26) because her neighbors and relatives would blame her for having a baby girl. One text of that period comments on the harsh ridicule directed toward women who gave birth to a girl and the frustration and anger leading to the practice of female infanticide: "Once they hear that someone's had a daughter, they say sharp and biting things, or they laugh behind her back, so that the birth mother burns up inside, and drowns the child in anger" (cited in King 2014, 26).

The social stigmatization of sonless families used to be prevalent in Lijia Village. According to elderly and middle-aged villagers, couples without a son were looked down on (*rangren kanbuqi*), considered inferior (*diren yideng*), could not hold their heads high (*taibuqitou*), and were even regarded as having a defect (*youquexian*). When a sonless villager had a verbal confrontation with other villagers, the person was often cursed with *juehou* and *duanzi juesun* (family line finished or ruined), the utmost humiliation to a family. A woman in her fifties who did not have a son told me that "when somebody said that I was *juehou*, I was so devastated." The stigma that was attached to sonless villagers suggests that full personhood could only be achieved through producing at least one son.

During my fieldwork in Lijia Village, however, the ability to continue the family line no longer served as the most significant marker defining individual identity and family status. Instead, as the story at the beginning of the chapter reveals, young Lijia villagers consider financial ability the most critical standard for social status. After the market reforms, rural communities became increasingly stratified in economic position, political power, and social status (Yan 2009). This stratification was first manifested in financial disparity. While villagers who were physically capable and hardworking were able to accumulate wealth by farming and engaging in nonagricultural employment, those who were physically less capable or whose family incurred major financial expenses fell to the lowest rung of the economic ladder in their community. With new consumption trends rapidly replacing earlier ones and the rising cost of childrearing and wedding financing, strong financial abilities allowed a family to acquire trendy consumer goods, support a child's education and finance a son's marriage, and build a social network. Consequently, economic stratification led to the differentiation in social status.

A family with strong financial abilities can keep up with the latest fashions in consumption and leisure activities. As discussed in chapter 2, young villagers pursue consumer goods for status recognition. Strong purchasing power demonstrates a couple's status as capable consumers and modern villagers who lead the consumption trends in their community. The purchase of a major household item, such as a desktop computer or a refrigerator, would give a couple a sense of pride; their relatives and friends would visit to check out their new purchase and perhaps follow their choice. Even engaging in leisure activities requires an income. A middle-aged Lijia woman told me: "If you don't have money, people don't even want to play mahjong with you [for fear that you will not be able to pay if you lose]." Strong financial ability also allows a couple to fulfill their parental responsibility, such as supporting a child for a college education and financing a son's wedding. As costs have skyrocketed in recent years, a couple usually has to borrow money from their friends and relatives to finance a son's wedding. The ability of a family to pay for a son's wedding without asking for too much help is highly admired, whereas couples, who are unable to provide the money or who require large loans are looked down on as lazy and irresponsible parents. A young Lijia woman told me about the experience of her husband's brother and sister-in-law, who had to rely on their relatives to help finance their son's wedding, "They [the brother and sister-in-law] felt so embarrassed to borrow a large amount of money from their relatives that they kept postponing their visits to ask for loans. Eventually, my husband took his nephew to visit each relative and ask for money. How embarrassing!"

Finally, with strong financial abilities families are able to produce and strengthen social networks. Since decollectivization, rural residents have relied heavily on their networks for economic assistance in areas such as agricultural production and personal financing, social support during life crises and at life-cycle rituals, and political support and alliance (Kipnis 1997; Yan 1996). Personal networks extend beyond a person's patrilineal kinsmen, and affinal relatives and friends have become increasingly significant. Families with strong financial abilities are often the most desirable for network building because they have financial resources that could be valuable for other villagers in need. A Lijia woman told me: "During farming seasons, when we need to hire labor, we have to ask people for help. The wealthy families do not even need to ask. People go to ask them if they need workers. People want to make friends with families who have money, because when they need money, they can ask for help from their wealthy friends."

A Lijia man explained the shift from having sons to having strong financial ability as the most significant marker for status and prestige: "In the past, if you had sons, you had everything. Nowadays, you have everything only if you have money." To explain, he shared a story he had seen on television: "A wealthy landowner wanted to show off his wealth to his friend. He invited the friend for dinner and put four gold ingots under the four table legs. Feeling insulted, the next day, the friend returned the favor and invited the wealthy man for dinner. This friend had four sons, and he asked his sons to kneel down under the table, each carrying one leg on his back." While amused at the story, he continued: "This is what people believed in the past. Having sons was more important than wealth. Now it's just the opposite."

In the past, wealth was one of the markers for status and prestige within a community. In the strong patrilineal tradition, however, having at least one male heir was considered indispensable. Wealthy families who had not produced a son had the financial resources to try other options, such as polygyny and adoption, to secure a male heir (Bray 2009). Thus, family continuity could be achieved through financial means. In pre-1949 Chinese society, wealth went hand in hand with family continuity and defined the status of a family. In contemporary Lijia Village, financial status has become increasingly significant in a family's pursuit of competitive consumption, support for a child's education and marriage, and social network building. When the institutional support for having a son is almost nonexistent and the belief in ancestor worship is weak, wealth eventually replaces family continuity through sons as the ultimate marker defining the status of a family and an individual.

With the changing criteria for status in the village, negative public opinion about families without a son has relaxed. I asked several couples who had a singleton daughter whether they had ever been cursed as *juehou*. None of them had nor had they heard of anyone who had been insulted with the word in recent years. One woman said: "I don't have a son. So what? Some families in the village have a son, but they can't even afford nice clothes for their children." Another woman told me: "If someone were to curse me with *juehou*, I would say 'It's not that I'm not able to have a son. I just don't want to!'"

## Conclusion

Without the presence of a lineage culture, there is no institutional support or pressure for having a son to pass on the family line. Furthermore, skepticism about the existence of an afterlife and a reciprocal relationship between the ancestors and the living descendants has undermined the religious and cultural significance of having a son to perform ancestral rituals among many villagers. Finally, although families without a son used to be stigmatized by their community, the stigma has been removed as financial ability has become the most significant marker for social status. These three factors have jointly contributed to a weakening of the importance of having a son to continue the family line among young Lijia couples.

The drastic change in the long-standing preference for sons and the importance of family continuity in Chinese families has had a significant impact on the reproductive choice among young Lijia couples. While the older generation may still expect their sons and daughters-in-law to have a son to continue the family line, many young couples, emerging from the ancestors' shadow, no longer believe that having a son is necessary for lineage continuity, a secure afterlife, and personal identity and social status. Instead, they have willingly embraced a singleton daughter and reoriented their life goals, strengthening their financial standing through hard work so as to support their family and establish their status in their community.

# Conclusion

**THE PRECEDING CHAPTERS** have delved into the complex decision-making process of young couples who choose to have a singleton daughter so as to unravel the socioeconomic and cultural forces leading to the transformation of gendered reproductive preferences in China. First, the reorientation of life goals and changing childrearing strategies among young couples have contributed to the preference for a family with only one child. Furthermore, the transformation of the gendered practice of filial piety, the rising cost of financing a son's wedding, and the weakened belief in the importance of family continuity have resulted in a decline in the preference for a son. The interplay of these factors has led to a fundamental change in China's long-standing preference for multiple children with at least one male heir among them. This chapter looks at the implications of this emerging reproductive pattern in relation to the transformations of the Chinese family in general and son preference in particular. The chapter also discusses the roles of state population control and the reproductive wishes and choices of young couples in China's recent fertility decline.

## Transforming the Chinese Family and Son Preference

China's deeply rooted preference for sons was sustained through the patrilineal kinship system, which promoted the father-son identification and the inherent discrimination against women. Under this kinship system, the Chinese family was organized to serve the elderly through filial support provided by sons and also to honor ancestors through ancestral rituals performed by male members. The decline of the sons' practices of filial piety and ancestor worship has significantly challenged the elderly-oriented patrilineal kinship system. Meanwhile, a new ideal of happiness for nuclear families and a practice of rearing an only child successfully have developed among young couples. With the emergence of "descending familism" among Chinese families (Yan 2016), family resources flow downward and "the focus of the existential meanings of life has shifted from the ancestors to the grandchildren" (245).

This shift from an elderly-oriented family model to a new emphasis on the nuclear family, and children in particular, can be illustrated by a doggerel verse composed by Lijia villagers in recent years: "There is a 'dad' in each family. You send him off in the morning and pick him up in the evening. At noon, you have to give him some pocket money" (*yijia yigedie / zaoshangson, wanshangjie / zhongwu haide geidian butie*). The rhyme vividly depicts the daily routine of parents sending a child to school, picking up the child after school, and providing the child with money for lunch. The "dad" is no longer the traditional patriarch in an extended family; instead, "dad" refers to the singleton child in a nuclear family, the "little emperor" (Jing 2000). The singleton child has thus eclipsed the preeminence of the elderly generation and has become the new focus of young parents.

The patriarchal gender relations inherent in the patrilineal kinship system have also been challenged by significant transformations in village life. Young married women have not only shouldered the responsibility for household chores and childcare but have also actively participated in the labor force. Because the pursuit of consumer goods and the desire for successful childrearing require a good income, their contribution to the family economy has become indispensable and has been highly valued by their husband. Moreover, as a result of the male-biased sex ratio in the marriage market and the responsibility of the groom's family for financing his wedding, young women have gained the upper hand in both forming and terminating a marriage. This has further contributed to their empowerment in marriage and family relations.

Young women's empowerment in marriage has undermined the

preference for a son. In the Chinese patrilineal and patriarchal tradition, producing at least one male heir secured a young bride's position in her husband's family. Today's young brides, however, have proven their worth even before marriage by exerting their power during the negotiation of marriage proposals. After marriage, they have been able to maintain their advantage with their husbands and in-laws. Although their husbands or in-laws may still expect them to pass on the family line, having sons no longer has a significant effect on women's status within their marriage or extended families. Additionally, with their newly gained power, women are able to exercise their agency in making their reproductive choices when their preference for a singleton daughter does not coincide with their husband's or in-laws' preferences.

Furthermore, a close bond between a daughter and her parents has been fostered. Married daughters have started to practice filial piety toward their parents and have become a valuable source of physical, emotional, and even financial support for them. Parents with an unmarried daughter have lavished love and affection on her and provided their wholehearted support for her daily consumption and education. The close parent-daughter bond and the unprecedented parental support and care for a daughter have significantly challenged the deeply rooted tradition of preference for sons and discrimination against daughters among Chinese families.

## State Population Control and Individual Reproductive Choice

After more than three decades of birth-planning enforcement, the total fertility rate of the world's most populous country has significantly declined. The "later, longer, fewer" population policy in the 1970s led to a dramatic drop in China's total fertility rate from 5.8 births per woman in 1970 to 2.3 in 1980 (Feng Wang 2011). In the early 1990s, fertility fell to below the replacement level (Cai 2010; Guo and Chen 2007). In about two decades, China achieved a fertility decline that had taken seventy-five years or longer to complete in Europe (Feng Wang 2011). In 2014 China's total fertility rate was between 1.5 and 1.65 births per woman, well below the replacement level (NHFPCPRC 2015). China has become a "demographic overachiever" in the global process of demographic transition (Feng Wang 2011).

The Chinese government has attributed the fertility decline to enforcement of the birth-planning policy, claiming that the policy had prevented four hundred million births (NHFPCPRC 2007). While the policy did accelerate the fertility decline, demographers have challenged the claim that the policy played a dominant role in China's drive to reach a below-replacement fertility rate (Cai 2010; Feng Wang 2011; Whyte, Wang, and Cai 2015). A demographic study of four rural regions in West and Central China selected for a pilot two-child policy beginning in the mid-1980s, surprisingly shows that in spite of a two-child policy, fertility rates in these regions were below the replacement level (Gu and Wang 2009). Recent studies on a similar fertility decline suggest that socioeconomic transformations were the key factors contributing to the decline (Cai 2010; Zheng et al. 2009).

Echoing the demographic studies on recent reproductive preferences in China, the Lijia case further reveals that choosing a singleton daughter is not a reluctant response to the birth-planning policy; rather, it is the result of a desire for only one child among individuals who wish to have a modern family and a successful child. In her research on reproductive preferences of Vietnamese women under a state family-planning program in the mid-1990s, Tine Gammeltoft (1999) found that women were confronted with two different objectives: following the state norm for a small family and meeting the family's need for additional children. While Vietnamese women acknowledged that the abstract state norm was good and necessary, the family's more concrete and specific desire carried more weight. In the Lijia case, young villagers' preference for a small family and acceptance of a singleton daughter coincided with the one-child state norm. Of course, the pervasive state campaign promoting small families and the value of girls has had a significant impact on young Lijia parents who came of age under the enforcement of the birth-planning policy. Even so, when young Lijia couples expressed their preference for a singleton daughter, they did not simply reiterate state propaganda on the benefits of a small family and the value of girls. Instead, they explained that their choice stems from their desire of attaining a new ideal of happiness, raising a successful child, and forming a close bond with a daughter.

In November 2015, China made the long-awaited announcement officially ending the one-child policy and allowing all couples to have two children. Although this historic revision of the policy did not change the persistence of a state-mandated birth limit in China, the welcome step gives a large number of Chinese couples the opportunity to have two children. With the ending of the one-child birth limit, the long-term demographic and social consequences of the one-child policy loom large: a growing aging population that requires financial support and nursing care, a skewed sex ratio that has created a surplus of men, and an increasing number of families who have lost an only child born under the one-child policy. As China moves forward with the new birth-planning policy, it will need to continue to address the growing pains that the policy has left behind.

# Character List

| | |
|---|---|
| bangganhuo | 帮干活 |
| buchi'er laoren | 不斥儿老人 |
| budani bumani | 不打你不骂你 |
| bure laoren shengqi | 不惹老人生气 |
| buda buma jiushi xiao | 不打不骂就是孝 |
| changhuijia kankan | 常回家看看 |
| chaosheng youjidui | 超生游击队 |
| chuxi | 出息 |
| cihou | 伺候 |
| dajihuang | 大饥荒 |
| dajihuang laile | 大饥荒来了 |
| dali tichang yidui fufu zhishengyu yigehaizi | 大力提倡一对夫妇只生育一个孩子 |
| daxi | 大喜 |
| dianji | 惦记 |
| diren yideng | 低人一等 |
| dusheng zinu guangrong zheng | 独生子女光荣证 |
| duanzijuesun | 断子绝孙 |
| dunuhu | 独女户 |
| erzi buxiao, youerzi yemeiyong | 儿子不孝，有儿子也没用 |
| erxifu chengle laopopo | 儿媳妇成了老婆婆 |
| funu zhuren | 妇女主任 |
| ganzhe | 干折 |
| geifanchi | 给饭吃 |

| | |
|---|---|
| geiqianhua | 给钱花 |
| geiqian dou bushengle | 给钱都不生了 |
| guigei erzi | 归给儿子 |
| guogangle | 过岗了 |
| guoji | 过继 |
| haimei wancheng renwu | 还没完成任务 |
| heihun | 黑婚 |
| heixin | 黑心 |
| huoren yanmu | 活人眼目 |
| huozhe buxiao sile luanjiao | 活着不孝, 死了乱叫 |
| huozhe weile xiangshou | 活着为了享受 |
| jihua shengyu zhengce | 计划生育政策 |
| jihua shengyu xianjin xiang | 计划生育先进乡 |
| jihuang | 饥荒 |
| jiehukoubende | 接户口本的 |
| juehou | 绝后 |
| kai xiaokou | 开小口 |
| kanjia | 看家 |
| kang | 炕 |
| kangshang deyou lashide, fenshang deyou shaozhide | 炕上得有拉屎的, 坟上得有烧纸的 |
| kaoziji | 靠自己 |
| kexin | 可心 |
| ke yige haizi peiyang | 可一个孩子培养 |
| lajihuang | 拉饥荒 |
| lianhuo buliancai | 连火不连财 |
| lianhuo liancai | 连火连财 |
| liangshou zhunbei | 两手准备 |
| menqian chema feiweigui, jiayou zisun busuanpin | 门前车马非为贵, 家有子孙不算贫 |
| mu | 亩 |
| naojin jiu | 脑筋旧 |
| naoxin | 闹心 |

| | |
|---|---|
| nuer shi diemade tiexin xiaomian'ao | 女儿是爹妈的贴心小棉袄 |
| nuren nengding duobanbiantian | 女人能顶多半边天 |
| pa erzi | 怕儿子 |
| pan erzi | 盼儿子 |
| peidu | 陪读 |
| peisong | 陪送 |
| quge xifu guochuquge erzi | 娶个媳妇过出去个儿子 |
| rangren kanbuqi | 让人看不起 |
| rensi rudengmie | 人死如灯灭 |
| sanjin | 三金 |
| shangfen shaozhide | 上坟烧纸的 |
| shaosheng yousheng, liguo limin | 少生优生, 利国利民 |
| shehui | 社会 |
| shengnu | 剩女 |
| siqing | 四清 |
| sixiang datong le | 思想打通了 |
| suidaliu | 随大流 |
| taibuqitou | 抬不起头 |
| taigu | 太孤 |
| tu | 土 |
| wan, xi, shao | 晚, 稀, 少 |
| weile guojia fuqiang, jiating, xingfu, qingnin jihua shengyu | 为了国家富强, 家庭幸福, 请您计划生育 |
| wenhua di | 文化低 |
| xiwang gongcheng | 希望工程 |
| xiangkai le | 想开了 |
| xiao | 孝 |
| xinchangre | 心肠热 |
| xincu | 心粗 |
| xinxi | 心细 |
| yang'er fanglao | 养儿防老 |
| yanghuo laoren | 养活老人 |
| yanglao baoxian | 养老保险 |

| | |
|---|---|
| yanglao nuxu | 养老女婿 |
| yipiao foujue | 一票否决 |
| yidui fufu yiduihai, lianghai xiangge siwunian | 一对夫妇一对孩，俩孩相隔四五年 |
| yijia yigedie, zaoshangson, wanshangjie, zhongwu haide geidian butie | 一家一个爹，早上送，晚上接，中午还得给点补贴 |
| yizhi laohu nenglanlu, shizhi haozi weimaochi | 一只老虎能拦路，十只耗子喂猫吃 |
| yougeban | 有个伴 |
| younengnai | 有能耐 |
| youquexian | 有缺陷 |
| youshengnan, meishengnu | 有剩男，没剩女 |
| zaguo maitie | 砸锅卖铁 |
| zaoshang sandianban, wanshang kanbujian | 早上三点半，晚上看不见 |
| zhangshang mingzhu | 掌上明珠 |
| zhuaqian | 抓钱 |
| zhuanyunzhu | 转运珠 |

# Appendix: Estimation of Annual Income of an Average Three-Person Nuclear Household in Lijia Village

There were two major sources of income in Lijia Village, income from farming and income from nonagricultural employment. Because the amount of land of each family was public knowledge and because all Lijia families farmed the same crop, annual income from farming could thus be calculated. For nonagricultural employment, I had obtained data on monthly salary of different types of jobs and the duration of the jobs. The following is an approximate amount of the annual income of an average three-person nuclear household in Lijia Village.

## Income from Farming:
The following is the record of the cost and the income from farming of a Lijia household with one couple and a singleton daughter in 2006.

Amount of land: 3.8 mu per person × 3 = 11.4 mu; total amount of corn harvested: 7,500 kg.

Cost of seeds:
  First purchase: ¥8 per kg × 20 kg = ¥160
  Second purchase: ¥10.8 per kg × 10 kg = ¥108
  Subtotal: 268 yuan
Cost of plowing:
  ¥16 per mu × 11.4 mu = ¥182.4
Cost of fertilizer:
  First purchase: ¥92 per bag × 5bags = ¥460
  Second purchase: ¥2 per kg × 25 kg = ¥50
  Third purchase: ¥93 per bag × 5 bags = ¥465
  Subtotal: ¥975
Cost of sowing:
  ¥10 per mu × 11.4 mu = ¥114
Cost of spreading pesticide:
  ¥150 yuan

Cost of hired labor to pick corn:

¥500

Cost of hired vehicles and labor to deliver corn stalks to home:

¥25 per truck load × 5 loads = ¥125

TOTAL COST: ¥2,314.4

INCOME FROM SELLING CORN: ¥1.16 per kg × 7,500 kg = ¥8,700

NET INCOME: ¥8,700 − ¥2,314.4 = ¥6,385.6

## Income from Nonagricultural Employment:

The amount of income from nonagricultural employment depended on the number of people who were engaged in employment in a household, the duration of the employment, and the type of employment. For example, in the brick kiln outside Lijia Village, based on the intensity of the labor, there were different tiers of monthly salary. In 2006, the highest amount of salary in the kiln was 1,500 yuan for delivering brick mud into extremely high-temperature kilns, whereas the lowest salary in the kiln was 400 yuan for covering and uncovering brick piles. The duration of employment in the brick kiln ranged between seven and eleven months a year, based on the type of job involved. During my fieldwork between 2006 and 2007, monthly salary typically ranged between 800 and 1,500 yuan for men and between 400 and 900 yuan for women.

Based on the above calculation, in 2006, for a three-person nuclear household, in which the husband was the only person engaged in a nonagricultural employment, the amount of annual income from farming and nonagricultural employment could range between 12,000 and 23,000 yuan. However, the highest amount was very difficult to achieve because very few men were physically strong enough to take highly labor-intensive jobs and because the majority of villagers were not able to work for eleven months a year due to health issues, family affairs, and circumstances related to the employment. It is also important to note that in 2006 villagers enjoyed perfect weather for farming and an increase of price for corn. The amount of net income from farming was much less in the previous years. Moreover, several young wives were not allocated any land after they moved into Lijia Village, and this had decreased the income from farming in those households. A conservative estimate of an annual income of an average three-person household in Lijia Village around 2006 could be more than 10,000 yuan. This estimate is supported by my interviews with Lijia villagers who agreed that for a household in which at least one person was engaged in a nonagricultural employment, annual income could reach more than 10,000 yuan in 2006.

# Notes

## Introduction

1. To protect the privacy of my informants, I use pseudonyms for the names of the village, the township, the county, and all of my informants.

2. According to the birth-planning policy, a couple whose child was certified to have congenital defects was allowed to have a second child. A couple who already had one child could divorce and arrange a marriage between the wife and a childless man. The birth-planning policy granted a couple a birth permit if one spouse did not have a child before the marriage. After the woman gave birth to a child, she could terminate her marriage and remarry her former husband. If the arrangement was not detected, the couple was able to have a second child without any financial penalty.

3. The alarmist argument has been critiqued as reinforcing problematic gender stereotypes and orientalist images of China (see Hartmann 2006; Ross 2010).

4. I only included long-term residents in the village. Some villagers kept their household registration in the village, but had permanently moved to other villages upon marriage. A few villagers moved to the county seat for employment opportunities. I did not include these villagers in my calculation. I included long-term residents whose household registration was not in Lijia Village. These villagers included women who moved out of Lijia Village upon marriage and later returned with their husband and children because it was closer to employment opportunities. For the number of households, elderly couples who shared a house with the family of a married son but were supporting themselves without financial help from their son's family were considered a separate household.

5. For a detailed account of agricultural collectivization in rural China, see Chan, Madsen, and Unger (2009); Hershatter (2011); Shu-min Huang (1998); Li (2009); and Ruf (1998).

6. In China, rural collectives have the ownership of agricultural land. Peasants have the land use right, which can be inherited.

7. In the winter, the majority of factories and construction sites where Lijia villagers work are closed because of the cold weather and the Lunar New Year holiday. Some

Lijia villagers seek other employment opportunities during the break, such as working temporarily for people who purchase agricultural products. Others take a break from work and stay at home.

## Chapter 1

1. For a detailed and comprehensive account of the formulation of China's birth-planning policy, see Greenhalgh (2008); Greenhalgh and Winckler (2005); Scharping (2003); and White (2006).

2. According to this modified policy, a couple needed to meet the following qualifications to have a second child: the husband and the wife held rural residency status, or the wife and the first child held rural residency status; and the first child was a daughter. The policy was first introduced in 1984 in limited rural areas and was further extended to most provinces by 1988, see Yi Zeng (1989). For a detailed discussion on the policy revision to allow couples whose first child was a girl to have a second child, also see Liang (2014).

3. The policy that allowed couples to have a second child if one spouse was a singleton child was initiated in Lijia Village and the county area in 2010.

4. In March 2013, the National Population and Family Planning Commission was merged with the former Ministry of Health into the National Health and Family Planning Commission.

5. A women's leader receives a salary for her work. For example, in 2006, the salary for this position was four thousand yuan a year. Given the yearly household income in Lijia Village, the salary for this position was desirable.

6. In a few villages that have a larger population size than Lijia Village, three assistants were assigned.

7. During the mid-1980s, the highest monthly salary for employment in the brick kiln was about five hundred yuan, about one third of the salary paid for the same job in 2006.

8. This policy was first enforced in several selected provinces in 2004. In 2015, Liaoning Province was included for this policy implementation (Ge 2006).

9. In rural China, land for housing is allocated by a village government according to the size of a household. Villagers can only build a house on their allocated land.

10. In each of these two cases, the woman left her husband and cohabited with another Lijia man. In each case, the couple would have been allowed to have a child if they had obtained a marriage certificate, because one of the partners did not have a child. Without a marriage certificate, neither couple was able to apply for a birth permit and their births were considered unauthorized.

11. See table 3 later in this chapter for data on sex ratio at second birth.

12. She gave birth to her second daughter before the relaxation of the one-child limit and the second birth was considered policy violation.

13. Some villagers bribed the officials for reduced fines for an early marriage. These

couples held a wedding ceremony and cohabited before they reached the legal age for marriage (twenty-two years for men and twenty for women). They would register their marriage later when they had reached the legal age. The government terms this practice *heihun* (illegal marriage). When an illegal marriage is reported, local government will impose a fine on the couple.

14. This couple was granted a second-child permit in 1986. However, they eventually decided not to have a second child. They told me that the major reasons for this decision were the wife's physical condition and the financial burden of raising a second child.

15. The number of applicants in 2005 was particularly high. My interviews with couples who applied for a one-child certificate that year reveal that some of them applied for a certificate because of a rumor that land would be reallocated soon and couples who had applied for a one-child certificate would be granted extra land. However, the rumor was never materialized.

## Chapter 2

1. For a detailed discussion on gendered division of farm work and unequal pay for men and women during the collective period, see Bossen (2002), Davin (1975), Hershatter (2011), Potter and Potter (1990), Stacey (1983), and Wolf (1985).

2. In rural Northeast China, villagers use a big iron wok for cooking. The wok is built into the stove, which is connected to a large bed (*kang*) in the bedroom made of bricks with air tunnels inside it. Thus, whenever villagers cook a meal in the wok, hot air travels through the air tunnels inside the bed and heats the kitchen and the bedroom. This efficient way of cooking a meal and simultaneously heating the room doesn't cost anything because the stoves are heated with corn stalks collected from the fields. On hot summer days, however, young villagers prefer to use an electric rice cooker and an electric stovetop and pay for electricity to avoid the heat from cooking in a wok.

3. Some women made fake eyelashes and decorative plastic butterflies and flowers at home for extra income.

4. Couples were unable to receive help with childcare from their parents-in-law when a mother-in-law had passed away, when the wife had conflicts with her parents-in-law, or when an elderly couple had multiple sons and was therefore unable to offer help to all sons and daughters-in-law.

5. Because Xu Hua had trouble with her IUD, she had it taken out and was not using any contraception. Because she and her husband were qualified for a second child, the women's leader did not require her to use contraception.

## Chapter 3

1. In the county senior high school, as well as in many prestigious schools in other regions of China, students whose scores for the entrance examinations are several

points lower than the cutoff for admission have the chance to pay extra tuition to be admitted as self-financed students.

2. Students from rural regions attending the top senior high schools in the county seat usually live on campus because of time constraints and the inconvenience of commuting. Public transportation between the school and Lijia Village ends in early evening, and a bicycle ride takes about forty minutes. For senior high school students who aim to go to college, every minute preparing for the entrance examination is precious. Living on campus frees them to concentrate on studying without losing time because of commuting. During a child's senior year in high school, some parents move close to the school so that their child can live with them and can be taken better care of.

3. In Chinese folk literature, a tiger is considered the king of all animals and is associated with power and strength. In contrast, a mouse is associated with weakness and timidity.

4. Yunxiang Yan's study of the cost of childrearing in Xiajia Village finds a new category of incidental expenses that includes toys and food items (2003, 206).

5. The side of the bed that is closest to the stove is often better heated than the other side.

6. In rural Guangdong, parents also made decisions on whether to continue supporting the child's education based on academic performance rather than the child's gender. See Oxfeld (2010, 97).

7. In her study of parental support for a daughter's education in Central China, Hong Zhang (2005) reveals that some parents had supported a daughter rather than a son because the daughter had shown greater potential for a college education.

8. As an exception, Ping-Chen Hsiung (2005, 203) reveals a father's affection toward a daughter during late imperial times.

## Chapter 4

1. There are exceptions, in areas where women's labor was highly valued in prerevolutionary China, when women maintained close ties with their natal families and made a contribution to their parents' old-age support. See Topley (1975), Siu (1993), and Stockard (1989). Some studies have documented the existence of an intimate bond between a daughter and her natal parents in postrevolutionary China as well. See Evans (2008); Fong (2004); Judd (1989, 1994).

2. Another major expense is a deceased parent's funeral. In Lijia Village, sons are responsible for the expense of the funeral services and a feast for guests after the funeral. Daughters pay for the expense of hiring a mourning band at the funeral. The son who holds the funeral feast also keeps the gift money received from guests. Therefore, in some cases in Lijia Village, several sons competed to hold a parent's funeral.

3. To join the rural cooperative medical system, villagers pay a small amount of

money into a cooperative fund. The Chinese government provides partial financial support for the fund, which covers a portion of medical treatment in designated hospitals for enrolled rural residents.

4. For detailed studies on sons' bargaining over their responsibilities of supporting elderly parents, see Cohen (1976) and Ikels (1993).

5. The obligation of adult children to provide financial support for needy parents is stipulated in Article 183 of the 1979 Criminal Law, Article 15 of the 1980 Marriage Law, and Article 49 of the 1982 Constitution. See Palmer (1995).

6. All interviews with the elderly parents were conducted privately, without the presence of their married children. Among the thirty-four informants fourteen were couples and were interviewed separately.

7. Some studies have also found an increase in filial practice of married daughters in China. See Miller (2004); Oxfeld (2010); Whyte (2004); Yan (2003); Zhan and Montgomery (2003).

8. Li Lan's biological parents were from a different village in the same township. They had planned to divorce when Li Lan was three months old and arranged for her to be adopted. After her adoption, she and her biological parents remained in contact. Her biological parents, who reconciled and remained married and had several more children, visited her several times; she visited them only once.

9. A study on gender differences in adult children's financial support to parents in urban China reveals that married daughters, especially those who live with their parents, provide more financial support to parents than married sons do. See Xie and Zhu (2009).

10. Elder-care insurance was recently introduced in Lijia Village. Only people under fifty were qualified for enrollment. The first person who purchased a policy was fifty-six years old in 2007.

11. In his research on adoption in a village in North China, Zhang Weiguo (2001) reveals that there have been more couples adopting a daughter than a son since the 1980s; a major contributing factor has been their belief in daughters' greater reliability for old-age support. For studies on parents' cultivating a close bond with daughters, see Yan (2003) and Hong Zhang (2005).

## Chapter 5

1. In Lijia Village, local term for debt is *jihuang*; borrowing money is called *la jihuang*. .

2. Out of twenty-five bachelors between twenty-six and fifty, except for three cases in which the man had a physical or mental defect and therefore had greater difficulty in finding a marriage partner, all had missed the most desirable age for marriage or were unable to find a partner for remarriage, mainly because their families were unable to finance a wedding for them.

3. Also see Yan (2003) for a thorough study of the transformation of the ownership of bridewealth in rural Northeast China.

4. In the mid-1970s, Lijia peasants worked in production teams under collective farming. Work for the production team was recorded as work points—for instance, ten points a day for a male laborer and eight points for a female laborer. The value of work points was calculated by dividing a production team's total income from selling corn to the state by the team members' total work points earned. Thus, depending on the productivity of each team and the number of work points earned, the value of every ten work points varied from 0.38 yuan to one yuan. A large proportion of income, however, was spent on grain and other types of food that the production team allocated each member, which left a household a very small amount of cash by the end of a year. For an estimate of annual income in 2006, see the appendix. Villagers told me that offering bridewealth in the mid-1970s was a financial burden for the majority of families. During that time, however, a well-built or newly renovated house for a young couple was not required. Thus, housing, coupled with other additional betrothal gifts and household items, has become the major contributing factor to the increasing burden of wedding financing.

5. Although the legal age for marriage in China is twenty for women and twenty-two for men, many young Lijia villagers begin to look for a marriage partner in their late teens. Once a marriage proposal is secured, a young couple will establish their conjugal household, following a wedding ceremony, the ritual that socially legitimizes a marriage. The couple would obtain a marriage certificate after both of them have reached the legal age for marriage.

6. In Xu Wei's girlfriend's village, forty thousand yuan was the newly requested, and accepted, amount of bridewealth at the time.

7. Wang Mei was working as a waitress in a restaurant in the city before she went home for the matchmaking. Her coworkers were from rural areas in neighboring counties.

8. Although villagers of her generation had not lived under Japanese colonial rule in Northeast China during the first half of the twentieth century, mainstream media reports and movie and TV drama portrayals of the Japanese invasion in China overwhelmingly present images of the brutality of Japanese soldiers and the suffering of Chinese civilians.

9. There were exceptions of women leaving their husbands during Han times. See Raphals (1998, 22).

10. The number does not include a few cases in which a bachelor over thirty either cohabitated with or legally married a divorced woman for a very brief time and had to terminate the relationship either because of frequent conflicts or marriage fraud, such as cases in which the woman left after securing bridewealth.

## Chapter 6

1. In 2007, the total cost of the Lunar New Year celebration for a nuclear family—including multiple meals, fruits, snacks, alcohol and other beverages, firecrackers, and New Year couplets—was between two hundred and three hundred yuan. Because the New Year's Eve dinner is most important, its cost took up a major portion of the total expenses. When a son's family had the dinner at the house of the husband's parents, the son's family usually contributed some money or food for the meal.

2. The ancestral tablets of couples without a son would be taken by a married daughter into her husband's family and placed on a shelf in a corner in the house. They would only be worshipped on certain occasions, such as Lunar New Year's Day, and not on their death anniversaries. Sonless couples had the option of arranging an uxori-local marriage for a daughter. After their deaths, they would be worshipped by their daughter and son-in-law. See Ahern (1973).

3. Some villagers wrote down the names of ancestors on the spirit money before burning it. Villagers believed that this would ensure that their ancestors in the underworld would receive it.

4. Although a few elderly villagers expressed to me a fear of cremation and a preference for burial after their deaths, villagers are required by the government to cremate their deceased family members. A crematorium is located about two kilometers from the village. Villagers bury the ashes on a small hill behind the village. Because the township government is located adjacent to Lijia Village, villagers are unable to secretly bury the bodies of family members for fear that officials in the township will find out. I was told, however, that in more remote villages, some villagers had secretly buried the bodies of family members.

5. In her study of death rituals in rural Guangdong, Ellen Oxfeld documents a similar saying that criticizes the practice of not being filial while parents were alive but putting on a grand show of worshipping them after their deaths (2010, 137).

6. Villagers believe that burning spirit money either in front of a grave or at a cross-road is a way to send offerings to ancestors.

# References

Adrian, Bonnie. 2006. Geographies of Style: Taiwan's Bridal Photography Empire. *Visual Anthropology* 19 (1): 73–85.

Ahern, Emily M. 1973. *The Cult of the Dead in a Chinese Village*. Stanford, CA: Stanford University Press.

Anagnost, Ann. 1995. Surfeit of Bodies: Population and the Rationality of the State in Post-Mao China. In *Conceiving the New World Order: The Global Politics of Reproduction*, edited by Faye D. Ginsburg and Rayna Rapp, 22–41. Berkeley: University of California Press.

Anderson, Siwan, and Debraj Ray. 2010. Missing Women: Age and Disease. *Review of Economic Studies* 77:1262–1300.

Attané, Isabelle, Zhang Qunlin, Li Shuzhuo, Yang Xueyan, and Christophe Z. Guilmoto. 2013. Bachelorhood and Sexuality in a Context of Female Shortage: Evidence from a Survey in Rural Anhui, China. *China Quarterly* 215:703–76.

Bai, Limin. 2006. Graduate Unemployment: Dilemmas and Challenges in China's Move to Mass Higher Education. *China Quarterly* 185:128–44.

Baker, Hugh D. R. 1968. *A Chinese Lineage Village: Sheung Shui*. Stanford: Stanford University Press.

———. 1979. *Chinese Family and Kinship*. New York: Columbia University Press.

Banister, Judith. 1987. *China's Changing Population*. Stanford, CA: Stanford University Press.

Bossen, Laurel. 2002. *Chinese Women and Rural Development: Sixty Years of Change in Lu Village, Yunnan*. Lanham, MD: Rowman and Littlefield.

Bray, Francesca. 2009. Becoming a Mother in Late Imperial China: Maternal Doubles and the Ambiguities of Fertility. In *Chinese Kinship: Contemporary Anthropological Perspectives*, edited by Susanne Brandstädter and Gonçalo D. Santos, 181–203. Abingdon, Oxon: Routledge.

Browner, C. H. 1986. The Politics of Reproduction in a Mexican Village. *Signs* 11 (4): 710–24.

Browner, Carole H., and Carolyn F. Sargent, eds. 2011. *Reproduction, Globalization, and the State: New Theoretical and Ethnographic Perspectives.* Durham, NC: Duke University Press.

Cai, Yong. 2010. China's Below-Replacement Fertility: Government Policy or Socioeconomic Development? *Population and Development Review* 36 (3): 419–40.

Cai, Yong, and William Lavely. 2007. Child Sex Ratio and Their Regional Variation. In *Transition and Challenge: China's Population at the Beginning of the 21st Century*, edited by Zhongwei Zhao and Fei Guo, 108–23. Oxford: Oxford University Press.

Carter, Anthony. 1995. Agency and Fertility: For an Ethnography of Practice. In *Situating Fertility: Anthropology and Demographic Inquiry*, edited by Susan Greenhalgh, 55–85. Cambridge: Cambridge University Press.

Chan, Anita, Richard Madsen, and Jonathan Unger. 2009. *Chen Village: Revolution to Globalization.* Third Edition. Berkeley: University of California Press.

Chee, Bernadine W. L. 2000 Eating Snacks, Biting Pressure: Only Children in Beijing. In *Feeding China's Little Emperors: Food, Children, and Social Change*, edited by Jun Jing, 48–70. Stanford, CA: Stanford University Press.

Chen, Junjie. 2011. Globalizing, Reproducing, and Civilizing Rural Subjects: Population Control Policy and Constructions of Rural Identity in China. In *Reproduction, Globalization, and the State: New Theoretical and Ethnographic Perspectives*, edited by Carole H. Browner and Carolyn F Sargent, 38–52. Durham, NC: Duke University Press.

Chu, Junhong. 2001. Prenatal Sex Determination and Sex-selective Abortion in Rural Central China. *Population and Development Review* 27 (2): 259–81.

Ci Qinying and Tian Yujie. 2004. Nongcun Dunuhu nanhai pianhao chuanhua yanjiu: Jiyu Hubei Bufen Xianshi deDiaocha [The study on the transformation of son preference among rural households with a singleton daughter: Based on a survey in several counties and cities in Hubei]. *Nanfang Renkou* [Southern Population] 19 (1): 9–15.

Cohen, Myron. 1976. *House United, House Divided: The Chinese Family in Taiwan.* New York: Columbia University Press.

———. 1992. Family Management and Family Division in Contemporary Rural China. *China Quarterly* 130:357–77.

———. 2005. *Kinship, Contract, Community, and State: Anthropological Perspectives on China.* Stanford, CA: Stanford University Press.

Collier, Jane Fishburne. 1997. *From Duty to Desire: Remaking Families in a Spanish Village.* Princeton, NJ: Princeton University Press.

Croll, Elisabeth. 1981. *The Politics of Marriage in Contemporary China.* Cambridge: Cambridge University Press.

———. 1994. *From heaven to Earth: Images and Experiences of Development in China.* London: Routledge.

———. 2000. *Endangered Daughters: Discrimination and Development in Asia.* London: Routledge.

————. 2006a. *China's New Consumers: Social Development and Domestic Demand.* London: Routledge.

————. 2006b. The Intergenerational Contract in the Changing Asian Family. *Oxford Development Studies* 34 (4): 473–91.

Davin, Delia. 1975 Women in the Countryside of China. In *Women in Chinese Society,* edited by Margery Wolf and Roxane Witke, 243–73. Stanford, CA: Stanford University Press.

Davis, Deborah, ed. 2000. *The Consumer Revolution in Urban China.* Berkeley: University of California Press.

Davis, Deborah S., and Julia S. Sensenbrenner. 2000. Commercializing Childhood: Parental Purchases for Shanghai's Only Child. In *The Consumer Revolution in Urban China,* edited by Deborah S. Davis, 54–79. Berkeley: University of California Press.

Davis, Deborah, and Stevan Harrell. 1993. Introduction. In *Chinese Families in the Post-Mao Era,* edited by Deborah Davis and Stevan Harrell, 1–22. Berkeley: University of California Press.

Du, Shanshan. 2011. Introduction: Toward Multiethnic Approaches to Women and Gender in Chinese Societies. In *Women and Gender in Contemporary Chinese Societies: Beyond Han Patriarchy,* edited by Shanshan Du and Ya-chen Chen, 1–31. Lanham, MD: Lexington.

Easterlin, Richard A. 1973. Relative Economic Status and the American Fertility Swings. In *Family Economic Behavior,* edited by Eleanor B. Sheldon, 170–227. Philadelphia: Lippincott.

Eastman, Lloyd E. 1988. *Family, Fields, and Ancestors: Constancy and Change in China's Social and Economic History, 1550–1949.* New York: Oxford University Press.

Ebrey, Patricia Buckley. 1991. *Confucianism and Family Rituals in Imperial China: A Social History of Writing about Rites.* Princeton, NJ: Princeton University Press.

Evans, Harriet. 2008. *The Subject of Gender: Daughters and Mothers in Urban China.* Lanham, MD: Rowman and Littlefield.

Fan, C. Cindy, and Youqin Huang. 1998. Waves of Rural Brides: Female Marriage Migration in China. *Annals of the Association of American Geographers* 8 (2): 227–51.

Fei, Hsiao-tung. 1939. *Peasant Life in China : A Field Study of Country Life in the Yangtze Valley.* New York: Dutton.

Fincher, Leta Hong. 2014. *Leftover Women: The Resurgence of Gender Inequality in China.* London: Zed.

Fong, Vanessa L. 2002. China's One-Child Policy and the Empowerment of Urban Daughters. *American Ethnologist* 104 (4): 1098–1109.

————. 2004. *Only Hope: Coming of Age under China's One-Child Policy.* Stanford, CA: Stanford University Press.

Freedman, Maurice. 1966. *Chinese Lineage and Society: Fukien and Kwangtung.* New York: Humanities.

————, ed. 1970. *Family and Kinship in Chinese Society*. Stanford, CA: Stanford University Press.

Friedman, Sara L. 2006. *Intimate Politics: Marriage, the Market, and State Power in Southeastern China*. Cambridge, MA: Harvard University Press.

Gammeltoft, Tine. 1999. *Women's Bodies, Women's Worries: Health and Family Planning in a Vietnamese Rural Community*. Richmond, Surrey, UK: Curzon.

Gates, Hill. 1993. Cultural Support for Birth Limitation among Urban Capital-Owning Women. In *Chinese Families in the Post-Mao Era*, edited by Debra Davus and Stevan Harrell, 251–76. Berkeley: University of California Press.

Ge Suhong. 2006. *Liaoning shishi nongcun bufeng jihua shengyu jiating jiangli fuzhu zhidu* [Liaoning Province implementing policy to award and help rural families who abided by the birth-planning policy]. February 11. http://chinaeast.xinhuanet.com/2006–02/11/content_6215895.htm.

Ginsburg, Faye, and Rayna Rapp. 1991. The Politics of Reproduction. *Annual Review of Anthropology* 20:311–43.

Gong Weigang, Chengrong Duan, and Hailong Wu. 2013. Zhongguo nongcun shengyu zhuanbian de leixing yu zongzu wenhua de quyu chayi China [Regional variation of lineage culture and fertility transition in cural China]. *Zhongguo xiangcun yanjiu* [China Rural Studies] 1:218–52.

Gottschang, Thomas R., and Diana Lary. 2000. *Swallows and Settlers: The Great Migration from North China to Manchuria*. Ann Arbor: Center for Chinese Studies, University of Michigan.

Greenhalgh, Susan. 1993. The Peasantization of the One-Child Policy in Shaanxi. In *Chinese Families in the Post-Mao Era*, edited by Debra Davis and Stevan Harrell, 219–50. Berkeley: University of California Press.

————. 1994. Controlling Births and Bodies in Village China. *American Ethnologist* 21 (1): 1–30.

————. 2008. *Just One child: Science and Policy in Deng's China*. Berkeley: University of California Press.

————. 2010. *Cultivating Global Citizens: Population in the Rise of China*. Cambridge, MA: Harvard University Press.

Greenhalgh, Susan, and Edwin A. Winckler. 2005. *Governing China's Population: From Leninist to Neoliberal Biopolitics*. Stanford, CA: Stanford University Press.

Gu Baochang and Feng Wang. 2009. *Babaiwan ren de shijian: Laizi erhai shengyu zhengce diqu de diaoyan baogao* [An experiment with eight million people: Report from regions with a two-child policy]. Beijing: Shehui kexue wenxian chubanshe [Social Sciences Academic Press].

Guo Yuhua. 2000. Family Relations: Generational Gap at the Table. In *Feeding China's Little Emperors: Food, Children and Social Change*, edited by Jun Jing, 94–113. Stanford, CA: Stanford University Press.

———. 2001. Daiji guanxi zhong de gongping luoji jiqi bianqian: dui Hebei nongcun yanglao shijian fenxi [The logic of fairness and its change in intergenerational relations: An analysis of cases of elderly support in rural Hebei]. *Zhongguo xueshu* [Chinese Scholarship] 4:21–54.

Guo, Zhigang, and Wei Chen. 2007 Below Replacement Fertility in Mainland China. In *Transition and Challenge: China's Population at the Beginning of the 21st Century*, edited by Zhongwei Zhao and Fei Guo, 54–70. Oxford: Oxford University Press.

Han, Hua. 2007. Under the Shadow of the Collective Good: An Ethnographic Analysis of Fertility Control in Xiaoshan, Zhejiang Province, China. *Modern China* 33:320–48.

———. 2009 Living a Single Life: The Plight and Adaptations of the Bachelors in Yishala. In *Chinese Kinship: Contemporary Anthropological Perspective*, edited by Susanne Brandtstadter and Gonçalo Santos, 48–66. London: Routledge.

Harrell, Stevan. 1993. Geography, Demography, and Family Composition in Three Southwestern Villages. In *Chinese Families in the Post-Mao Era*, edited by Debra Davis and Stevan Harrell, 77–102. Berkeley: University of California Press.

Hartmann, Betsy. 2006. *The Testosterone Threat: Sociobiology, National Security and Population Control*. http://popdev.hampshire.edu/projects/dt/pdfs/DifferenTakes_41.pdf.

Hershatter, Gail. 2011. *The Gender of Memory: Rural Women and China's Collective Past*. Berkeley: University of California Press.

Ho, David Y. F. 1987. Fatherhood in Chinese Culture. In *The Father's Role: Cross-Cultural Perspectives*, edited by Michael E. Lamb, 227–45. Hillsdale, NJ: Lawrence Erlbaum Associates Publishers.

Hsiung, Ping-Chen. 2005. *A Tender Voyage: Children and Childhood in Late Imperial China*. Stanford, CA: Stanford University Press.

Hsu, Francis L. K. 1948. *Under the Ancestors' Shadow: Chinese Culture and Personality*. New York: Columbia University Press.

Huang, Shu-min. 1998. *The Spiral Road: Change in a Chinese Village through the Eyes of a Communist Party Leader*. Boulder, CO: Westview.

Huang Tao and Liuqian Zhang. 2015. *Hubei nongcun dushengnu jinnian gaokao ke jiafen* [Singleton daughters from rural Hubei can receive extra points for college entrance exam this year]. March 23. http://news.cnhubei.com/xw/kj/201503/t3213674.shtml.

Huang Xinmei. 1994. Nongcun dunuhu fangci ertai zhibiao de qishi [The implications of giving up the opportunity for a second child among rural couples with a singleton daughter]. *Renkou yu Jihua shengyu* [Population and Family Planning] 3:45–46.

Huang, Yanzhong, and Dali L. Yang. 2004. Population Control and State Coercion in China. In *Holding China Together: Diversity And National integration in the Post-*

*Deng Era*, edited by Barry Naughton and Dali Yang, 193–225. Cambridge: Cambridge University Press.

Hudson, Valerie M., and Andrea M. den Boer. 2005. *Bare Branches: The Security Implications of Asia's Surplus Male Population*. Cambridge, MA: MIT Press.

Hvistendahl, Mara. 2011. *Unnatural Selection: Choosing Boys over Girls, and the Consequences of a World Full of Men*. New York: Public Affairs.

Ikels, Charlotte. 1993. Settling Accounts: The Intergenerational Contract in an Age of Reform. In *Chinese Families in the Post-Mao Era*, edited by Deborah Davis and Stevan Harrell, 277–333. Berkeley: University of California Press.

Jankowiak, William R. 1993. *Sex, Death, and Hierarchy in a Chinese City: An Anthropological Account*. New York: Columbia University Press.

———. 2002. Proper Men and Proper Women: Parental Affection in the Chinese Family. In *Chinese Femininities, Chinese Masculinities: A Reader*, edited by Susan Brownell and Jeffery N. Wasserstrom, 361–80. Berkeley: University of California Press.

———. 2011. The Han Family: The Realignment of Parenting Ideals, Sentiments, and Practices. In *Women and Gender in Contemporary Chinese Societies: Beyond Han Patriarchy*, edited by Shanshan Du and Ya-chen Chen, 109–32. Lanham, MD: Lexington Books.

Jankowiak, William R., and Robert L. Moore. 2017. *Family Life in China*. Malden, MA: Polity Press.

Jeffrey, Patricia, Roger Jeffrey, and Andrew Lyon. 1988. *Labour Pains and Labour Power: Women and Childbearing in India*. London: Zed.

Jilin Provincial Government. 2008. *Guanyu kaizhan nongcun dunuhu fufu yanglao baoxian shidian de zhidao yijian* [Guidelines on implementing a pilot program on Old-age support insurance among rural couples with a singleton daughter]. October 27.

Jiang Zhenghua. 2007. Quanguo renda changweihui fuweiyuanzhang Jiang Zhenghua zai guojia renkou fazhan zhanlue yanjiu gongzuo zongjie zuotanhui shang de jianghua [Speech at the roundtable on the report on the strategic study of China's population development by the vice chairmen of the standing committee of the National People's Congress of China], April 14, 2006. *Zhongguo renkou he jihuashengyu nianjian* [China population and family planning year book]. Edited by Zhongguo renkou he jihuashengyu nianjian weiyuanhui [China population and family planning committee], 17–20. Beijing: China Population and Family Planning Year Book Press.

Jing, Jun, ed. 2000. *Feeding China's Little Emperors: Food, Children, and Social Change*. Stanford, CA: Stanford University Press.

Johnson, Kay Ann. 1996. The Politics of the Revival of Infant Abandonment in China, with Special Reference to Hunan. *Population and Development Review* 22 (1): 77–98.

————. 2016. *China's Hidden Children: Abandonment, Adoption, and the Human Costs of the One- Child Policy.* Chicago: University of Chicago Press.

Johnson, Kay, Huang Banhan, and Wang Liyao. 1998. Infant Abandonment and Adoption in China. *Population and Development Review* 24 (3): 469–510.

Jordan, David K. 1972. *Gods, Ghost, and Ancestors: The Folk Religion of a Taiwanese Village.* Berkeley: University of California Press.

Judd, Ellen R. 1989. Niangjia: Chinese Women and Their Natal Families. *Journal of Asian Studies* 48 (3): 525–44.

————. 1994. *Gender and Power in Rural North China.* Stanford, CA: Stanford University Press.

Kanaaneh, Rhoda Ann. 2002. *Birthing the Nation: Strategies of Palestinian Women in Israel.* Berkeley: University of California Press.

King, Michelle. 2014. *Between Birth and Death: Female Infanticide in Nineteenth-Century China.* Stanford, CA: Stanford University Press.

Kipnis, Andrew. 1997. *Producing Guanxi: Sentiment, Self, and Subculture in a North China Village.* Durham, NC: Duke University Press.

————. 2011. *Governing Educational Desire: Culture, Politics, and Schooling in China.* Chicago: University of Chicago Press.

————. 2016. *From Village to City: Social Transformation in a Chinese County Seat.* Oakland: University of California Press.

Kligman, Gail. 1998. *The Politics of Duplicity: Controlling Reproduction in Ceausescu's Romania.* Berkeley: University of California Press.

Knapp, Keith. 2005. *Selfless Offspring: Filial Children and Social Order in Medieval China.* Honolulu: University of Hawai'i Press.

Kuan, Teresa. 2015. *Love's Uncertainty: The Politics and Ethics of Child Rearing in Contemporary China.* Oakland: University of California Press.

Lavely, William. 1991. Marriage and Mobility under Rural Collectivism. In *Marriage and Inequality in Chinese Society*, edited by Rubie S. Watson and Patricia Buckley Ebrey, 286–312. Berkeley: University of California Press.

Lee, James, and Cameron Campbell. 1997. *Fate and Fortune in Rural China: Social Organization and Population Behavior in Liaoning, 1774–1873.* Cambridge: Cambridge University Press.

Lee, James, and Wang Feng. 1999. *One Quarter of Humanity: Malthusian Mythology and Chinese Realities, 1700– 2000.* Cambridge: Harvard University Press.

Li, Huaiyin. 2009. *Village China under Socialism and Reform: A Micro-History, 1948–2008.* Stanford, CA: Stanford University Press.

Liang Zhongtang. 2014. *Zhongguo jihua shengyu zhengce shilun* [History of China's birth-planning policy]. Beijing: Zhongguo fazhan chubanshe [China Development Press].

Liu Min and Hong Ding. 1993. Dui 1.8wan dunvhu ziyuan fangqi ertai shengyu zhibiao de diaocha yu sikao [The study on 18 thousand households with a singleton daughter who voluntarily gave up a second-child quota]. *Renkou yu jihua shengyu* [Population and Family Planning] 6:60–61.

Liu, Shao-hua. 2011. *Passage to Manhood: Youth Migration, Heroin, and AIDS in Southwest China*. Stanford, CA: Stanford University Press.

Liu, Xin. 2000. *In One's Own Shadow: An Ethnographic Account of the Condition of Post-Reform Rural China*. Berkeley: University of California Press.

Lo, Yuet Keung. 2004. Filial Devotion for Women: A Buddhist Testimony from Third-Century China. In *Filial Piety in Chinese Thought and History*, edited by Alan K. L. Chan and Sor-hoon Tan, 71–90. London: RoutledgeCurzon.

Loh, Charis, and Elizabeth J. Remick. 2015. China's Skewed Sex Ratio and the One-Child Policy. *China Quarterly* 222:295–319.

Ma, Guoqing. 2002. The Recreation and Production of Tradition: The Revival of Lineage and Folk Beliefs in a Field Survey of Zhanghu Town in Northern Fujian Province. *Chinese Sociology and Anthropology* 34 (3): 69–91.

Miller, Eric T. 2004. Filial Daughters, Filial Sons: Comparisons from Rural North China. In *Filial Piety: Practice and Discourse in Contemporary East Asia*, edited by Charlotte Ikels, 34–52. Stanford, CA: Stanford University Press.

Milwertz, Cecilia Nathansen. 1997. *Accepting Population Control: Urban Chinese Women and the One-Child Family Policy*. Richmond, Surrey, UK: Curzon.

Mitsuyoshi, Yoshie. 2012. Maternalism, Soviet-Style: The Working "Mothers with Many Children" in Post-war Western Ukraine. In *Maternalism Reconsidered: Motherhood, Welfare and Social Policy in the Twentieth Century*, edited by Marian van der Klein, Rebecca Jo Plant, Nichole Sanders and Lori R. Weintrob, 205–26. New York: Berghahn.

Mu Guangzhong, Mincai Zhang, Jun Jiang, Xianjun Pan, Wen Liu, and Yi Hong. 2009. Xinshiqi renkou yisheng gongzuo gaige yu fazhan yanjiu: Yi Liaoning sheng Liaoyang shi weili [The study on the reform and development of population and family planning work in the new era: An example from Liaoyang, Liaoning]. *Renkou yu fazhan* [Population and Development] 15(3): 67–75.

Mueggler, Erik. 2001. *The Age of Wild Ghosts: Memory, Violence, and Place in Southwest China*. Berkeley: University of California Press.

Mungello, D. E. 2008. *Drowning Girls in China: Female Infanticide since 1650*. Lanham, MD: Rowman and Littlefield.

Murphy, Eugene T. 2001. Changes in Family and Marriage in a Yangzi Delta Family Community 1930–1990. *Ethnology* 40 (3): 213–35.

Murphy, Rachel. 2003. Fertility and Distorted Sex Ratios in a Rural Chinese County: Culture, State, and Policy. *Population and Development Review* 29 (4): 595–626.

———. 2007. Paying for Education in Rural China. In *Paying for Progress in China: Public Finance, Human Welfare and Changing Patterns of Inequality*, edited by Vivienne Shue and Christine Wong, 69–95. London: Routledge.

Murphy, Rachel, Ren Tao, and Xi Lu. 2011. Son Preference in Rural China: Patrilineal Families and Socioeconomic Change. *Population and Development Review* 37 (4): 665–90.

Naftali, Orna. 2016. *Children in China*. Cambridge, UK: Polity Press.

National Bureau of Statistics of the People's Republic of China (NBSPRC). 2007. *Tabulation of the 2005 National 1% Population Sample Survey*. Beijing: China Statistics Press.

———. 2016. *2015 nian guomin jingji yunxing wenzhongyou jin wenzhong youhao* [In 2015 national economy is stable and growing]. January 19. http://www.stats.gov.cn /tjsj/zxfb/201601/t20160119_1306083.html.

National Health and Family Planning Commission of People's Republic of China (NHFPCPRC). 2007. *Report on the National Strategy of Population and Development*. January 11. http://www.gov.cn/gzdt/2007–01/11/content_493677.htm.

———. 2015. *Records of News Conference from National Health and Family Planning Committee*. July 10. http://www.nhfpc.gov.cn/xcs/s3574/201507/43685ecd0edb4b71b 260306af9b7e924.shtml

Nie, Yilin, and Robert J. Wyman. 2005. The One-Child Policy in Shanghai: Acceptance and Internalization. *Population and Development Review* 31 (2): 313–36.

Obendiek, Helena. 2017. Higher Education, Gender, and Elder Support in Rural Northwest China. In Transforming Patriarchy: Chinese Families in the Twenty-First Century, edited by Gonçalo Santos and Stevan Harrell, 74–90. Seattle: University of Washington Press.

Ownby, David. 2002. Approximations of Chinese Bandits: Perverse Rebels, Romantic Heroes, or Frustrated Bachelors? In *Chinese Femininities Chinese Masculinities: A Reader*, edited by Susan Brownell and Jeffery N. Wasserstrom, 226–20. Berkeley: University of California Press.

Oxfeld, Ellen. 2010. *Drink Water, But Remember the Source: Moral Discourse in a Chinese Village*. Berkeley: University of California Press.

Palmer, Michael. 1995. The Re-emergence of Family Law in Post-Mao China. *China Quarterly* 141:110–35.

Parish, William L., and Martin King Whyte. 1978. *Village and Family in Contemporary China*. Chicago: University of Chicago Press.Patel, Tulsi. 1999. The Precious Few: Women's Agency, Household Progressions and Fertility in Rajasthan Village. *Journal of Comparative Family Studies* 30:429–51.

Peng, Yusheng. 2011. When Formal Laws and Informal Norms Collide: Lineage Networks versus Birth Control Policy in China. *American Journal of Sociology* 116 (3): 770–805.

Potter, Sulamith Heins, and Jack M. Potter. 1990. *China's Peasants: The Anthropology of a Revolution*. Cambridge: Cambridge University Press.

Raphals, Lisa. 1998. *Sharing the Light: Representations of Women and Virtue in Early China*. Albany: State University of New York.

Rawski, Evelyn S. 1986. The Ma Landlords of Yang-chia-kou in Late Ch'ing and Re-publican China. In *Kinship Organization in Late Imperial China 1000–1940*, edited by Patricia Buckley Ebrey and James L. Watson, 245–273. Berkeley: University of California Press.

Ross, Kaz. 2010. An "Army of Bachelors"? China's Male Population as a World Threat. *Journal of Asian Pacific Studies* 1 (2): 338–63.

Ruf, Gregory A. 1998. *Cadres and Kin: Making a Socialist Village in West China, 1921–1991*. Stanford, CA: Stanford University Press.

Santos, Gonçalo. 2017. "Multiple Mothering and Labor Migration in Rural South China." In *Transforming Patriarchy: Chinese Families in the Twenty-First Century*, edited by Gonçalo Santos and Stevan Harrell, 91–110. Seattle: University of Washington Press.

Sargent, Carolyn F. 2006. Reproductive Strategies and Islamic Discourse: Malian Migrants Negotiate Everyday Life in Paris, France. *Medical Anthropology Quarterly* 20 (1): 31–49.

Sargeson, Sally. 2004. Building for the Future Family. In *Chinese Women—Living and Working*, edited by Anne E. McLaren, 149–168. London: RoutledgeCurzon.

Scharping, Thomas. 2003. *Birth Control in China 1949–2000: Population Policy and Demographic Development*. New York: RoutledgeCurzon.

Scott, James. 1985. *Weapons of the Weak: Everyday Forms of Peasant Resistance*. New Haven, CT: Yale University Press.

Sen, Amartya. 1990. More Than 100 Million Women Are Missing. *New York Review of Books* 37 (20).

Shi, Lihong. 2014. Micro-Blogs, Online Forums, and the Birth-Control Policy: Social Media and the Politics of Reproduction in China. *Culture, Medicine and Psychiatry* 38:115–32.

———. 2017. The New Rich and Their Unplanned Births: Stratified Reproduction under China's Birth-Planning Policy. *Medical Anthropology Quarterly* (forthcoming).

Shi, Yaojiang, and John James Kennedy. "Delayed Registration and Identifying the 'Missing Girls' in China." *China Quarterly* (2016) 228: 1018–38.

Siu, Helen. 1993. Reconstituting Dowry and Brideprice in South China. In *Chinese Families in the Post-Mao Era*, edited by Deborah Davis and Stevan Harrell, 165–88. Berkeley: University of California Press.

Stacey, Judith. 1983. *Patriarchy and Socialist Revolution in China*. Berkeley: University of California Press.

Stockard, Janice. 1989. *Daughters of the Canton Delta: Marriage Patterns and Economic Strategies in South China, 1860–1930*. Stanford, CA: Stanford University Press.

Szonyi, Michael. 2002. *Practicing Kinship: Lineage and Descent in Late Imperial China*. Stanford, CA: Stanford University Press.

Tai Shize and Kejian Li. 2015. *Huangping: jisheng liyi daoxiang zhengce zhu nongcun "li-*

*anghu" xuezi yuan shengxuemeng* [Huangping City: Policy granting benefits to rural students from "two types of households" enter college]. June 5. http://www.gz .xinhuanet.com/2015-06/05/c_1115526180.htm.

Tan, Sor-Hoon. 2004. Filial Daughters-in-law: Questioning Confucian Filiality. In *Filial Piety in Chinese Thought and History*, edited by Alan K. L. Chan and Sorhoon Tan, 226–40. London: RoutledgeCurzon.

Tan, Lin, and Susan E. Short. 2004. Living as Double Outsiders: Migrant Women's Experiences of Marriage in a County-Level City. In *On the Move: Women and Rural-to-Urban Migration in Contemporary China*, edited by Arianne M. Gaetano and Tamara Jacka, 151–76. New York: Columbia University Press.

Tang Zhaoyun. 2005. *Dangdai zhongguo renkou zhengce ranjiu* [The study of contemporary population policy in China]. Beijing: Zhishi chanquan chubanshe [Intellectual Property Rights Press].

To, Sandy. *China's Leftover Women: Late Marriage among Professional Women and Its Consequences*. London: Routledge, 2015.

Topley, Marjorie. 1975. Marriage Resistance in Rural Kwangtung. In *Women in Chinese Society*, edited by Margery Wolf and Roxanne Witke, 67–88. Stanford: Stanford University Press.

Tsui, Ming, and Lynne Rich. 2002. The Only Child and Educational Opportunity for Girls in Urban China. *Gender and Society* 16 (1): 74–92.

Waltner, Ann. 1990. *Getting an Heir: Adoption and the Construction of Kinship in Late Imperial China*. Honolulu: University of Hawai'i Press.

Wang, Danyu. 2004. Ritualistic Coresidence and the Weakening of Filial Practice in Rural China. In *Filial Piety: Practice and Discourse in Contemporary East Asia*, edited by Charlotte Ikels, 16–33. Stanford, CA: Stanford University Press.

Wang, Fei-Ling. 2005. *Organizing through Division and Exclusion: China's Hukou System*. Stanford, CA: Stanford University Press.

Wang, Feng. 2011. The Future of a Demographic Overachiever: Long-Term Implications of the Demographic Transition in China. *Population and Development Review* 37 (supp.): 173–90.

Wasserstrom, Jeffery. 1984. Resistance to the One-Child Family. *Modern China* 10 (3): 345–34.

Watson, James. 1975. Agnates and Outsiders: Adoption in a Chinese Lineage. *Man* 10 (2): 293–306.

———. 1986. Anthropological Overview: The Development of Chinese Descent Groups. In *Kinship Organization in Late Imperial China 1000–1940*, edited by Patricia Buckley Ebrey and James L. Watson, 274–92. Berkeley: University of California Press.

———. 1988. The Structure of Chinese Funerary Rites: Elementary Forms, Ritual Sequence, and the Primacy of Performance. In *Death Ritual in Late Imperial and*

*Modern China*, edited by James L. Watson and Evelyn S. Rawski, 3–19. Berkeley: University of California Press.

———. 2004. Self-Defense Corps, Violence, and the Bachelor Sub-Culture in South China: Two Case Studies. In *Village Life in Hong Kong: Politics, Gender, and Ritual in the New Territories*, edited by James L. Watson and Rubie S. Watson, 251–65. Hong Kong: Chinese University Press.

Watson, Rubie S. 1986. The Named and the Nameless: Gender and Person in Chinese Society. *American Ethnologist* 13 (4): 619–31.

———. 2004. Chinese Bridal Laments: The Claims of a Dutiful Daughter. In *Village Life in Hong Kong: Politics, Gender, and Ritual in the New Territories*, edited by James Watson and Rubie S. Watson, 221–250. Hong Kong: Chinese University Press.

White, Tyrene. 2006. *China's Longest Campaign: Birth Planning in the People's Republic, 1949–2005*. Ithaca, NY: Cornell University Press.

Whyte, Martin King. 2004. Filial Obligations in Chinese Families: Paradoxes of Modernization. In *Filial Piety: Practice and Discourse in Contemporary East Asia*, edited by Charlotte Ikels, 106–27. Stanford, CA: Stanford University Press.

Whyte, Martin King, Wang Feng, and Yong Cai. 2015. Challenging Myths about China's One-Child Policy. *China Journal* 74:144–59.

Wolf, Arthur P., and Chieh-shan Huang. 1980. *Marriage and Adoption in China, 1845–1945*. Stanford, CA: Stanford University Press.

Wolf, Margery. 1972. *Women and the Family in Rural Taiwan*. Stanford: Stanford University Press.

———. 1985. *Revolution Postponed: Women in Contemporary China*. Stanford, CA: Stanford University Press.

Woo, Margaret Y. K. 2006. Contesting Citizenship: Marriage and Divorce in the People's Republic of China. In *Sex and Sexuality in China*, edited by Elaine Jeffreys, 62–81. London: Routledge.

Xie, Yu, and Haiyan Zhu. 2009. Do Sons or Daughters Give More Money to Parents in Urban China? *Journal of Marriage and Family* 71(1): 174–86.

Yan, Yunxiang. 1996. *The Flow of Gifts: Reciprocity and Social Networks in a Chinese Village*. Stanford, CA: Stanford University Press.

———. 2003. *Private Life under Socialism: Love, Intimacy, and Family Change in a Chinese Village 1949–1999*. Stanford, CA: Stanford University Press.

———. 2009. *The Individualization of Chinese Society*. New York: Berg.

———. 2016. Intergenerational Intimacy and Descending Familism in Rural North China. *American Anthropologist* 118 (2): 244–57.

Yang, Keming, and Christina R. Victor. 2008. The Prevalence of and Risk Factors for Loneliness among Older People in China. *Aging and Society* 28:305–27.

Yuen, Sun-pong, Pui-lam Law, and Yuk-ying Ho. 2004. *Marriage, Gender, and Se in a Contemporary Chinese Village*. Armonk, NY: Sharpe.

Zeng, Yi. 1989. Is the Chinese Family Planning Program "Tightening Up"? *Population and Development Review* 15 (2): 333–37.

Zeng, Yi, Tu Ping, Gu Baochang, Xu Yi, Li Bohua, and Li Yongping. 1993. Causes and Implications of the Recent Increase in the Reported Sex Ratio at Birth in China. *Population and Development Review* 19 (2): 283–302.

Zhan, Heying Jenny, and Rhonda J. V. Montgomery. 2003. Gender and Elder Care in China: The Influence of Filial Piety and Structure Constraints. *Gender and Society* 17 (2): 209–29.

Zhang, Hong. 2004. "Living Alone" and the Rural Elderly: Strategy and Agency in Post-Mao Rural China. In *Filial Piety: Practice and Discourse in Contemporary East Asia*, edited by Charlotte Ikels, 63–87. Stanford, CA: Stanford University Press.

———. 2005. Bracing for an Uncertain Future: A Case Study of New Coping Strategies of Rural Parents under China's Birth Control Policy. *China Journal* 54 (2): 53–76.

———. 2007. From Resisting to "Embracing?" The One-Child Rule: Understanding New Fertility Trends in a Central China Village. *China Quarterly* 192:855–75.

Zhang, Jun, and Peidong Sun. 2014. "When Are You Going to Get Married?" Parental Matchmaking and Middle-Class Women in Contemporary Urban China. In *Wives, Husbands, and Lovers: Marriage and Sexuality in Hong Kong, Taiwan, and Urban China*, edited by Deborah S. Davis and Sara L. Friedman, 118–46. Stanford, CA: Stanford University Press.

Zhang, Li. 2010. *In Search of Paradise: Middle-Class Living in a Chinese Metropolis*. Ithaca, NY: Cornell University Press.

Zhang, Weiguo. 2001. Institutional Reforms, Population Policy, and Adoption of Children: Some Observations in a North China Village. *Journal of Comparative Family Studies* 32 (2): 303–318.

———. 2002. *Chinese Economic Reforms and Fertility Behavior: A Study of a North China Village*. London: China Library.

———. 2006. Who Adopts Girls and Why? Domestic Adoption of Female Children in Contemporary Rural China. *China Journal* 56:63–82.

Zhao Wuqiang. 2014. *Tongliang: 497ming nongcun dushengnu ke xiangshou gaokao jiafen zhengce* [Tongliang City 497 rural singleton daughters enjoy the policy that grants extra points to their college entrance exam]. June 14. http://cq.people.com .cn/news/2014614/201461411389688231.htm.

Zheng, Zhenman. 2001. *Family Lineage Organization and Social Change in Ming and Qing Fujian*. Translated by Michael Szonyi. Honolulu: University of Hawai'i Press.

Zheng, Zhenzhen, Yong Cai, Wang Feng, and Gu Baochang. 2009. Below-Replacement Fertility and Childbearing Intention in Jiangsu Province, China. *Asia Population Studies* 5 (3): 329–347.

Zheng Rong. 2004. Zhejiang lin'anshi shengyu wenhua bianqian de diaocha yu yanjiu: Guanyu zhejiangsheng lin'anshi 556tdui shuangnong dunuhu de diaocha yu fenxi [The study on the transformation of the fertility culture in Lin'an, Zhejiang: A study on 5,561 singleton daughter households in Lin'an, Zhejiang]. *Xibei renkou* [Northwest Population] 4 (98): 50–56.

Zhou Changhong and Jianfang Zhou. 2001. Woguo nongcun shengyu guannian zhuanbian de yige zhongyao biaozhi: Yichang shi nongcun faqi yu tuichi erhai shengyu xianxiang chengyin fenxi [A significant mark of the transformation of childbearing preference among peasants: A study on the causes of rural couples giving up or postponing having a second child in Yichang]. *Renkou yanjiu* [Population Research] 25 (1): 70–74.

# Index

Page numbers followed by f or t indicate material in figures or tables.